Troubled Times
for American
Higher Education

SUNY Series
FRONTIERS IN EDUCATION
Philip G. Altbach, Editor

The Frontiers in Education Series draws upon a range of disciplines and approaches in the analysis of contemporary educational issues and concerns. Books in the series help to reinterpret established fields of scholarship in education by encouraging the latest synthesis and research. A special focus highlights educational policy issues from a multidisciplinary perspective. The series is published in cooperation with the Graduate School of Education, State University of New York at Buffalo.

Class, Race, and Gender in American Education
—Lois Weis (ed.)

Excellence and Equality: A Qualitatively Different Perspective on Gifted and Talented Education
—David M. Fetterman

Change and Effectiveness in Schools: A Cultural Perspective
—Gretchen B. Rossman, H. Dickson Corbett, and William A. Firestone

The Curriculum: Problems, Politics, and Possibilities
—Landon E. Beyer and Michael W. Apple (eds.)

The Character of American Higher Education and Intercollegiate Sport
—Donald Chu

Crisis in Teaching: Perspectives on Current Reforms
—Lois Weis, Philip G. Altbach, Gail P. Kelly, Hugh G. Petrie, and Sheila Slaughter (eds.)

The High Status Track: Studies of Elite Schools and Stratification
—Paul William Kingston and Lionel S. Lewis (eds.)

Troubled Times for American Higher Education: The 1990s and Beyond

—Clark Kerr

Higher Education Cannot Escape History: Issues for the Twenty-first Century

—Clark Kerr

Troubled Times for American Higher Education:

The 1990s and Beyond

Clark Kerr

in association with

Marian L. Gade

and

Maureen Kawaoka

State University of New York Press

Published by
State University of New York Press, Albany

© 1994 State University of New York

For information, address State University of New York
Press, State University Plaza, Albany, N.Y. 12246

Production by M. R. Mulholland
Marketing by Fran Keneston

Library of Congress Cataloging-in-Publication Data

Kerr, Clark, 1911–
   Troubled times for American higher education : the 1990s and
beyond / Clark Kerr, in association with Marian L. Gade and Maureen
Kawaoka.
      p.   cm. — (SUNY series, frontiers in education)
   Includes bibliographical references and index.
   ISBN 0-7914-1705-0. — ISBN 0-7914-1706-9 (pbk.)
   1. Education, Higher—United States—Aims and objectives.
2. Education, Higher—Social aspects—United States.   3. Education,
Higher—Economic aspects—United States.   I. Gade, Marian L., 1934–
. II. Kawaoka, Maureen.   III. Title.   IV. Series.
LA227.4.K47 1993
378.73—dc20
                                                            92-47354
                                                            CIP
10 9 8 7 6 5 4 3 2 1   Rev

To Howard Bowen, who had the vision of a
"nation of educated people"

Man is born into trouble.

—Book of Job

Contents

Prologue: A New Age for Higher Education

The century now passing was a significantly American century in world history, as the United States became the dominant economy, the dominant military power, and the dominant intellectual power. Only two other political groupings in Western history ever were such preponderant forces in their times—the British empire in the nineteenth century and Greco-Roman civilization in the ancient world. And not since the Greeks has any single group of intellectuals so influenced new thought (particularly scientific) as Americans did in the second half of the twentieth century.

Higher education was a particular triumph. The United States came to lead in research and scholarship in the sciences and social sciences—although to a much lesser extent in the humanities and the arts. The U.S. system of higher education came to be the first to provide universal access, with financial support to students to make this access a practical reality. It responded with more alacrity and precision to the needs of the labor market than any such system had ever done before. No other system of higher education has ever performed, all around, so well.

Now we face the twenty-first century. A multipolar world is developing in the economic arena, and also in higher education. Two competitive areas, in particular, will be challenging American higher education—the more-united European Community and Japan. Both of these areas will have greatly augmented financial and intellectual resources for their institutions of higher education. No longer will the United States be able to be so unconcerned with developments elsewhere, as it has been in recent decades. The overall prospects for the next century are not that higher education in the United States will lose absolutely—in fact it is likely to gain substantially—but that other systems will rise comparatively. The United States may well remain first for the dimly foreseeable future, but first among more nearly equals.

Anticipating the future is always hazardous and often foolhardy, but as Charles Kettering once said: "We should all be concerned about the future because we shall have to spend the rest of our lives there." I shall be concerned here mostly with possibilities for the "medium-run" future, defined as the period during which substantial numbers of the current faculty will, in decreasing degree, still be active and influencing developments, and that is the period 1990–2010.

The overwhelming fact for the future of higher education is that it is ever more central to the evolution of American society. Thus it faces new horizons of service and a constantly new agenda. A new age for higher education is being born where it has, at one and the same time, more to do for society but less in the way of prospective additional resources to do it with. This may lead some to fear a Hobbesian world of "everyone against everyone," and some of the external and internal battles may become more intense in the prospective new "time of troubles," but doomsayers about American higher education have always been subject to some disappointment. American higher education will, I feel certain, once again demonstrate its great resiliency.

Nevertheless, I do see ahead "troubled times," as the title of this book states. This prospect both surprises and disturbs me. Howard Bowen[1] and I used to joke with each other that we were the only two optimists left about the future of American higher education. We felt this way in the 1970s and 1980s when so many thought that all was lost, and, in particular, we both were convinced (and history confirmed our convictions) that the then-prospective "demographic depression" was greatly exaggerated. I thought that Howard had deserted me, however, when he and Jack Schuster wrote *American Professors: A National Resource Imperiled;*[2] that he had become too pessimistic; that he had left me alone as the last of the optimists. Now I seem to have joined him in deserting optimism, although my concerns about the future are rather different from his.

The approach of the twenty-first century attracts added attention to prospects for the future. It is unlikely that any explosion of enrollments in higher education will ever again occur as in the twentieth century: from 240,000 in 1900 to an estimated 15.9 million in 2001. But changes will continue, although nothing now seems to lie ahead comparable to the period of the "Great Transformation" from 1960 to 1980.[3] The 1980s, by comparison, were tame. The 1990s, however, are already shaping up as a period of many tensions and conflicts.

The first series of essays that follows (Part I) looks at possible "contours" of the future and at "choices to be made" by higher education, with particular attention to how they may impact leadership by presidents and trustees. Part II concentrates on the relations between higher education and the health of the economy, a relationship that is currently of great importance but, in my judgment, overemphasized. Part III looks at some of the problems now emerging that may influence the near future.

This volume is presented in association with Marian L. Gade and Maureen Kawaoka. It has been prepared with their essential participation, as have been also so many other reports, books, and articles I have had a role in producing over the past nearly quarter century, including my years with the Carnegie Commission[4] and the Carnegie Council[5] on Higher Education, and the several reports under the auspices of the Association of Governing Boards of

Universities and Colleges[6] and the Education Commission of the States.[7] Marian, as research associate, and Maureen, as executive secretary, have at all times been the most pleasant and effective of colleagues, always willing to undertake any assignment and always able to fulfill it to perfection.

This is the second in a series of three volumes undertaken on the initiative and with the good advice of Philip G. Altbach.[8]

Notes

1. See Clark Kerr, "Howard R. Bowen (1908–1989): *Fiat Lux et Justitio Omnibus,*" *Change* 22, no. 2 (March-April 1990): 78–79.

2. Howard R. Bowen and Jack H. Schuster, *American Professors: A National Resource Imperiled* (New York: Oxford University Press, 1986).

3. Clark Kerr, *The Great Transformation in Higher Education: 1960–1980* (Albany: State University of New York Press, 1991).

4. Carnegie Commission on Higher Education, *A Digest and Index of Reports and Recommendations: December 1968–June 1972* (Berkeley: Carnegie Commission on Higher Education, 1972).

5. Carnegie Foundation for the Advancement of Teaching, *The Carnegie Council on Policy Studies in Higher Education: A Summary of Reports and Recommendations* (San Francisco: Jossey-Bass, 1980).

6. National Commission on Strengthening Presidential Leadership (Clark Kerr, Director), *Presidents Make a Difference* (Washington, D.C.: Association of Governing Boards of Universities & Colleges, 1984); Clark Kerr and Marian L. Gade, *The Many Lives of Academic Presidents: Time, Place, and Character* (Washington, D.C.: Association of Governing Boards of Universities & Colleges, 1986); and Clark Kerr and Marian L. Gade, *The Guardians: Boards of Trustees of American Colleges and Universities* (Washington, D.C.: Association of Governing Boards of Universities & Colleges, 1989).

7. Task Force on State Policy and Independent Higher Education (John Ashcroft and Clark Kerr, CoChairs), *The Preservation of American Higher Education: The Essential Role of Private Colleges and Universities* (Denver: Education Commission of the States, 1990).

8. Kerr, *Great Transformation;* and Clark Kerr, *Higher Education Cannot Escape History: Issues for the Twenty-first Century* (Albany: State University of New York Press, 1994).

PART I

Approaching the Twenty-first Century

Introduction: Approach with Caution

Higher education in the United States, after the status quo decade of the 1980s, faces perhaps two decades of greater changes and challenges. The chapters that follow seek to look at some of the possibilities ahead.

Chapter 1 is concerned with prospective "contours" that may affect the context within which higher education conducts its efforts.

Chapter 2 treats some of the "choices" that may need to be made as higher education attempts to influence the course of its future.

Chapter 3 notes that the prospective "contours" and "choices" particularly impact on leadership—on boards of trustees, on presidents, and on faculty leaders. They, in particular, will be on the firing lines and under greater threats of hostilities.

In looking at the future of higher education in the United States, it may be helpful to look also at the trends in other countries. What is happening in several or many other countries may represent more basic trends than what is happening in only one country. I advance this series of such fundamental and nearly universal developments:[1]

Financial resources from governments are more difficult to obtain. This reflects both the reduction by about one-half across the industrialized nations in the annual increase in productivity, which is the basic source of such resources, and the fact that higher education is by now a much heavier burden on resources.

Institutions of higher education are losing their intellectual independence as they become both more nearly an arm of the state and an arm of industry.

Governments are generally coming to rely more on general guidance of institutions of higher education than on line-item controls. Part of this guidance involves efforts to place these institutions under competitive market pressures in obtaining resources. Higher education is becoming more and more a market economy.

Governments are guiding higher education more in the direction of applied research, of applications of research, and of polytechnic skill training, and away from "pure scholarship." More research and more skill training is taking place outside higher education, as a related development. These tendencies reflect intensified worldwide economic competition.

Governments are also increasingly interested in enlarging opportunities for mass, and even universal, access to higher education.

The general trend is toward differentiation of functions among institutions as a response to the trend from elite to mass to universal access functions. But pressures for homogenization continue to exist, and the ultimate resolution in some countries is still in doubt.

Institutions, in response to some of the above developments, are becoming more entrepreneurial, with the president as chief entrepreneur.

They are also turning more to tuition from students as a source of funds. This requires the development of more-effective student aid systems.

Their curricular provisions are putting more emphasis on basic mathematical and language skills, and on the study of world civilizations.

The "brain drain" (or mobility of persons with high competence) is intensifying within as well as among nations.

Institutions of higher education are ever more concerned with their future prosperity and even survival—which can no longer be so taken for granted.

Internally, there is a decline in general citizenship responsibilities and an increase in fractionalization of interests.

Generally, public policy is concentrating on the advancement of practical interests within society while some elements of the campuses, on the contrary, are intensifying their emphasis on the passions attached to alternative views of desirable social conduct—with possible points of conflict in the course of this disjunction.

The United States, given the composition of its population, differs from other nations, in particular, in higher education's emphasis on affirmative action in admissions of students and additions of faculty members, and on multiculturalism in the curricula. Otherwise world and national trends are much the same.

Notes

1. This list is based in part on my notes on the discussions at the conference "The University of the Twenty-first Century" held at the University of Chicago, October 1991, under the chairmanship of Edward A. Shils, on the occasion of the celebration of the centennial of its founding.

CHAPTER 1

Contours of the Future for American Higher Education:
Aspects of Mature Development

I see ahead no third great transformation to match the periods after the War between the States or the two decades from 1960 to 1980.[1] But I do see shifting trends and developments that will induce changes that will write an interesting history in the future.

The biggest issues at the time of the first great transformation (1860 to 1890) were the reorientation of higher education to more forms of service to more elements of the population, and the replacement of a religious by a scientific orientation. The two biggest issues of the second transformation (1960 to 1980) were the explosion of student numbers, and the political unrest among students and faculty members. Four big long-term issues I now see ahead are the eternal issue of merit versus equality, the impacts of new orientations of knowledge, the changing mentalities of faculties and students related to social and political identifications, and a scarcity of resources and intensified competition for their allocation.

Near Certainties

There are no certainties.

—H. L. Mencken

Higher education in the United States has some well-established patterns of behavior that are likely to continue:

1. The secular trend in attendance rates. Higher education has responded to the ever-advancing proportion of the population wishing to attend institutions of higher education. Enrollment was, as a percentage of the 18–21 age cohort, as follows:

3 percent in 1890
16 percent in 1940

30 percent in 1950

40 percent in 1990 (50 percent attend at some point in their lives)

This trend will continue for the foreseeable future but almost certainly at a falling rate of progression. This long-run trend, however, was strong enough to help offset the long-heralded "demographic depression" of the 1980s, and its potential influence was mostly grossly underestimated in advance. Enlargement of the demand to fill the growing proportion of jobs in the labor market requiring a college education, rising per-capita wealth, and the growing impact of emulation as college attendance has become more the norm rather than the exception all support this secular trend. Possible future attendance rates might be as follows:

About 50 percent in 2000, to meet the estimated needs of the labor force for new entrants. (See chapter 4.)

60 percent in 2013, if Daniel Bell's scenario comes true as attendance reflects the expected increasing needs of the labor force.[2]

53 percent in 2030, if the trend from 1950 to 1990 continues, but this period included the transition from mass- to universal-access higher education, and this transformation will never be repeated.

54 percent in some still-distant future, if, as the Carnegie Council once suggested, the high school graduation rate for the nation comes to match the current rate in Minnesota (and also in Japan—90 percent) and if the college attendance rate of high school graduates for the nation comes to match that now in California (60 percent).

Approaching 100 percent ultimately, if Howard Bowen's dream of a nation of educated people really comes true.[3]

2. Changing size and age composition of the population. The future totality of enrollments will also be affected by the total size of the population, which is expected to remain fairly stable. It will additionally be affected by the changing age distribution, which is expected to continue to shift to older age groups. Higher education will probably continue to depend more and more on older students, but thus far this has meant mostly those under the age of thirty-five. Moreover, the age distribution of the population will continue to be affected, in diminishing degree, by the repercussions of the "baby boom" after World War II for at least another fifty years. Faculty recruitment patterns will also continue to reflect the changing size and age compositions of the population, to an exaggerated degree, up and down.

3. Shifts in racial and ethnic composition of the population. College attendance will also be affected by the composition of the total population by race and ethnic group. Minority Americans will prospectively be as follows as a percentage of the total population as compared with 1990:[4]

20 percent in 1990
30 percent in 2000
45 percent in 2050

In 1990, these minorities, on an overall basis, attended higher education at about two-thirds to three-fourths of the rate of the majority population. Presumably attendance will rise gradually toward majority levels. Higher education, for both of these reasons (minorities as an ascending percentage of the population and rising attendance rates among these minorities), will inevitably be more and more concerned with racial and ethnic issues than ever before, and also with remedial education.

Changing participation by gender will have much less impact than over the past half century, now that women attend at a slightly higher rate than men—except at the graduate level in general[5] and the higher-paid professional fields in particular.

4. *The fluctuating rates of payoff to higher education.* Both total numbers of students and their distribution among vocational fields will continue to respond rapidly and quite precisely to rates of payoff to higher education calculated as the excess of earnings of college graduates over high school graduates. These rates fluctuate quite rapidly. For males they were, overall,[6]

48 percent in 1969
38 percent in 1979
64 percent in 1989

The 1979 rate was depressed by the combination of a large supply of college graduates as the "tidal wave" of students entered the labor market and by a series of recessions that lowered demand. The higher rate of 1989 is more likely to indicate prospects for the near future, particularly as the demand to fill jobs requiring college-level education continues to increase, as some noncollege jobs are down-skilled, and as the infusion of new and less-educated immigrants puts downward pressure on rates of pay for non-college-level jobs.[7]

The collection and analysis of data for estimating these rates should be refined and followed closely in total, and field by field.

The above four considerations taken together indicate that, in terms of enrollments, the higher education system is entering a period of maturity with a slower growth rate than over the past century; but that it is not, as far as can now be foreseen, approaching a period of decline—far from it. The big impacts will come from the changing proportions of now-underserved minorities (and from the resultant big conflicts also), the aging of the population, and changing rates of payoff.

These forces affecting educational demographics give a portrait of mature development.[8] So also do the five other developments that follow next in our consideration of prospects for the future.

Probabilities

I see several areas where it appears that the historically developed situation has stabilized:

5. Massification. The greatest growth in the size of campuses is in the past. Average campus enrollment rose from less than one hundred in 1870 to fifteen hundred in 1950 to four thousand in 1990. Size for most types of institutions has risen beyond the level of any further clear gains in declining per-unit costs.[9] The burdens of increased impersonal bureaucratization have intensified. Many departments in large universities have passed the size of maximum effectiveness in relations among faculty colleagues.

6. Unionization. The rapid extension of unionization (1965 to 1975) is not likely to occur again. The most favored campuses for unionization have already come under contracts. These contracts have resulted more in advancing the doctrine of seniority than in fulfilling hopes for comparatively higher pay. The union movement, as a whole, is in retreat nationwide. Conditions for faculty members are likely to improve, or at least not deteriorate, in the academic marketplaces of the medium-term future.

7. The private sector. The private sector may well have settled out at about 20 percent of total enrollments. Enrollments on an absolute basis have stabilized since the late 1970s at 2.5 million. The loss in percentage of total enrollments (50 percent in 1950) was due to the very rapid growth of the public sector, which is not likely to occur again in the foreseeable future. There have been internal changes within the private sector, however, and particularly a decline in Liberal Arts II colleges.[10] The contributions of the private sector have been very substantial, and public policy has increasingly recognized this.[11]

8. Electronic technology. The new electronic technology may continue to advance modestly in its influence in the conduct of administration and research, but very slowly in teaching. In teaching, it will not result, as once prophesied, in a new revolution like that of five hundred years ago with the invention of printing.[12]

9. Shared governance. The broad sharing of governance will probably continue, at the formal level, about as it is in its multipolar configurations and perhaps rigidify in its details:

The state will control mostly the assignment of missions and the bulk of the financing in the public sector. State coordination, it is increasingly being recognized, works better when it takes the form of guidance of missions and financing by grants for broad purposes than when it attempts line-item control.

The market will control student choices of campuses and fields of study.

The faculty guild will control most academic decisions but, perhaps, with a change of spirit. If faculty members continue to withdraw from committee work, as they have been doing recently, then more responsibility for academic decisions will come to rest, in fact if not in the rules, with department chairs, deans, provosts, and presidents. Shared governance, however, works best with shared work, including by faculty members.

The president and the trustees will control most institutional housekeeping, provide coordination among all participants, and influence the directions and rates of changes.

But the high tide of the most effective shared governance may now be passing, if faculty participation at the committee and departmental levels continues to decline. If this happens, it will be greatly regrettable.

The Changing Map of Learning and Consequences for Higher Education

The developments thus far discussed generally favor stability, but some additional ones imply more dynamic change.

10. The advancement of specialized and vocational courses—the supremacy of the labor market. The distribution of students by fields within higher education will continue to follow the demands of the labor market, as it has increasingly over the past century. Until about 1820, undergraduate enrollments were concentrated nearly 100 percent in courses of general education; today that figure lies somewhere in the range of 30 to 35 percent.[13] This range is not likely to rise, even with demands for more attention to liberal education—which, in my judgment, are both a laudable goal and a likely fantasy in terms of substantial realization. The big changes in internal distribution by fields have been, and may continue to be, within the vocational orbit—the great gainers in recent times have been business administration, electrical engineering, and computer sciences.

11. The force of knowledge. New knowledge and new skills are now more important to the advance of civilization worldwide than ever before in the economy, in the polity, and in cultural areas. Thus, the higher education system, contributing as it does to new knowledge and new skills, becomes a more important system among the several systems that comprise society. This means ever more emphasis on research, on skill training, on service to productive elements of society—with leadership increasingly being shared by the United States with Europe and Japan. New knowledge is now the greatest single driving force around the world.

12. Shifts in areas of new knowledge. Within new knowledge, attention keeps shifting—in recent times to electronics (including computers), new sources of energy and energy conservation, new types of materials (including ceramics), biotechnology, and the environmental sciences, among others. And new methodologies, based on mathematics and statistics, are penetrating more and more fields, including the social sciences and even the humanities. Mathematics takes the place of philosophy as the most central department on campus—more central even to philosophy itself. This increasing emphasis on mathematics goes back, however, at least to Pythagoras.

13. The globalization of learning. Knowledge increasingly is being distributed worldwide, and not only scholars but also students in their curricula respond to the globalization of learning. Particularly at the curricular level, this process, outside the sciences, is at an early stage of development. I am now more receptive, however, than I once was to the conviction of Robert Maynard Hutchins that at some time in the future all students around the world will be taught the same subject matter, but I think that possibility is in a much more distant time than he thought.[14]

Consequences of these thirteen forces and developments affecting higher education can be dramatic. I shall concentrate on four.

Consequences for Higher Education

1. Expansion of functions. Expansion of functions for higher education will continue and will include

a. more remedial work
b. more concern for the youth group at large—partly because of the immensity of the problems and partly through the default of other elements of society
c. more cultural training and more public cultural programs for an older, better educated, and richer population
d. more efforts at applied research and at transmission of research into applications
e. more research into the social problems of society[15]
f. more organized thought about the great problems of the present and the future.

2. Changing locations for expanded functions. Changes in institutional configurations will continue. They will include more comparative attention (1) to community colleges, but also (2) to research universities and (3) to polytechnic training at all levels; and (4) to a continued expansion of "corporate classrooms" and of for-profit trade schools.[16]

3. The intensifying struggle over resources. The competition for scarce resources will intensify. This will occur, first of all, because higher education will require more resources. Second, there will be more competitors for public resources, including for assistance to the more-numerous elderly and the more-numerous neglected children. Third, resources will be in restricted supply if, as seems likely, the working-age proportion of the total population contracts, and the increase in per-capita productivity of the work force continues to hold at lower than historic levels—perhaps at 1 or 1.5 percent, rather than 2 to 3 percent, per annum.

This all means that both public and private institutions will need to look more actively, as they are already doing, at nonpublic sources of support. These include gifts and tuition. Tuition is a particular problem for public institutions, with their historic policies of low tuition. Additionally, the tuition burden will fall more and more on students and less on parents. Parents have been moving in a more hedonistic direction, spending more on themselves and less on the education of their children. Public support, thus far, has offset the decline of parental support and has grown greatly in the proportion of all expenditures on higher education. As further growth of public contributions becomes more difficult, however, the contest between parental versus student financing will increase. The students will lose. Thus loan programs to students will become increasingly important, with loan programs calling for more-assured repayment. Students are, it should be noted, the great beneficiaries of a college education, and they now, heavily subsidized as they are, are given great advantages over their age-cohort counterparts who do not go to college.

This is not to suggest that the states will not do their best. Their record at the time of the student troubles was remarkable. Looking at their contributions, one would never know that student troubles had alienated the public—but apparently only from the student activists and not from colleges and universities.

Partisan politics has had less impact on higher education in the United States than in some other countries—this has also been true, but to a lesser extent, of the United Kingdom and Canada. In continental Europe, state intervention, from a socialist and social democratic orientation, was massive in response to student revolts, as in France, Italy, Germany, Sweden, and the Netherlands, among others.[17] The emphasis was on equalization: of student access, of distribution of power in internal governance, and of status among institutions.

In the United States, such partisan influence has been only marginal and often nonexistent. Democrats have been somewhat more concerned with student access, and Republicans with research activity and with the welfare of private institutions. But there has been at least as much variation among Democrats and among Republicans as between them. The largely nonpartisan support for higher education in the United States has been a great asset in the past and is likely to continue into the future.

4. *Continuing conflicts.* Conflicts will continue over

a. comparative emphasis on merit versus equality as both become more important—the first, in economics, the second in politics
b. differentiation versus the homogenization of functions among institutions of higher education
c. governance reliance on general direction versus specific controls.

Clear Uncertainties with Unclear Consequences— Palpitations of the Heart

1. *Citizenship responsibilities—nomads and tribes.* The decline in devotion to and performance of citizenship responsibilities by faculty members on campus may (or may not) continue at a modest (or accelerated) rate, as rewards continue to be given more for other contributions and for seniority,[18] and as the "me generation" of self-gratification and personal cost-benefit analysis increasingly dominates the professoriate. These changes in performance of citizenship responsibilities include greater reluctance to serve on academic committees.[19] They also include more willingness to engage in economic, political, and academic exploitation of institutions of higher education—individual aggrandizement before campus welfare. The "wild card" is that we do not yet know how far these trends will go, whether or not they might be reversed, and what their full repercussions may be.

Henry Rosovsky, in his final report as dean of the Faculty of Arts and Sciences (FAS) at Harvard, wrote so very sadly:

This brings me to the crux of the matter. FAS has become a society largely without rules, or to put it slightly differently, the tenured members of the faculty—frequently as *individuals*—make their own rules. Of course, there are a great many rules in any bureaucratic organization, but these largely concern less essential matters. When it concerns our more important obligations—faculty citizenship—neither rule nor custom is any longer compelling.

To put it slightly differently, as a social organism, we operate without a written constitution and with very little common law. That is a poor combination, especially when there is no strong consensus concerning duties and standards of behavior.[20]

A related uncertainty is a continuing slow decline in the internal life of the campus as one integrated community.[21] Faculty members now live in more worlds than the campus alone, and so do their spouses, as they are more likely to be employed. The campus, particularly in the dominant public sector, is also less likely to be, and to view itself as, a self-governing unit of burghers.

Additionally, the campus, as also the external society, is becoming more a series of enclaves divided by race/ethnic group, by gender, by political orientation, by "old-guard" citizens versus "guest workers" whose basic allegiances lie elsewhere.

The declines in citizenship participation and in sense of community strike me as the most important developments affecting academic life today. In the academic world, as elsewhere, more people are acting like nomads—moving from place to place, living off the land; and like members of tribes contending with each other.[22]

2. *Student (and faculty) political activism.* A second (and partially related) "wild card" is the prospect for student (and faculty) political unrest—a possible repetition of the 1930s or 1960s. In the long run, the tendency has been toward recurrence of periods of such unrest at heightened levels of intensity from one to the next. I have doubts that this history will continue to repeat itself, or, at least, repeat itself in the same way. The new political issues of race and gender are more likely to set student group against student group and faculty group against faculty group than to set students and faculty, together, against the campus administration or the external society. Societal issues are moving from a vertical plane to the horizontal—from the poor against the rich, from the powerless versus the powerful, from the workers against the capitalists, in vertical opposition, to more-horizontal conflicts of black or brown versus white, of male versus female, of pro-choice versus pro-life, of environmentalists versus developers, of cultural conformists versus adherents to the counter culture, of pro- versus anti- this or that "exploited" group or special cause around the world. A single unified "movement" or "revolution" now seems less likely in the future than it seemed in the past. On campus, as within the nation, horizontal tribal warfare at least partially replaces class or antiestablishment vertical warfare in one form or another.[23]

The forms of warfare that may best fit this fractionalization of protest are small scale and guerilla-type actions of an anarcho-syndicalist orientation by special interest groups, more like the IWW of World War I and the early 1920s than the "old Left" of the 1930s or "*the* movement" of the 1960s. In the 1930s, the "old Left" advanced the idea of "*the* revolution" to end all revolutions; in the 1960s, the "new Left" supported "*the* movement" that was to "reconstitute" the university and then, through the university, the society. Now the emphasis is more on spontaneous acts of protest, issue by issue, regarding, for example, policy toward South Africa or toward Iraq, with varying coalitions forming and dissolving.

The experience of the Rutgers conference in February 1988 is informative. It involved seven hundred political activists from 130 campuses. The intent was to establish a new "united front of the left." The result was "catastrophe."[24] The conference broke wide open. The basic split was between black and Third World students versus majority students. But this was not just a split based on racial/ethnic status. It also involved goals: more social justice for minorities versus a total reconstruction of society. It also involved means: "how best to mobilize campus and community" for practical results versus a more "hyper-militant late-sixties" approach. And were individuals to be involved for the sake of their ideological interests or for the sake of the "desire to prove commitment" and to experience "heroic militancy"?

Activists are now more divided by goals. They are also more divided by means: negotiation and persuasion, or peaceful civil disobedience, or enticement of police violence, or directly initiated violence? And there exists an overall conflict of whether to try to revive the "mythic character of the sixties," or to learn from the earlier "limited success" of "a movement that had somehow gone awry," and then build their own "alternative political models."

How will it all turn out? We cannot know. My own expectation is that there will be more fractionalization over goals than in the earlier part of the 1960s, and a reemergence of the fractionalization over means that became so controversial in the late 1960s. I anticipate that there will be segmented issues and an occasional overarching current event issue with temporary coalitions but no one "movement" or "revolution"; and more emphasis on the nonviolent within the spectrum of means than on the violent, as a result of reflections on the counterproductive emphasis on violence in the late sixties.

3. Changing mentalities. In the 1960s, a major theme was dissent and experimentation; in the 1970s and 1980s, it was more self-gratification—each with impacts on higher education. What mentalities may develop in the future is sheer speculation. One possibility is that there will be still more development in the direction of individual nomads and of more tribal groupings, as discussed above.

Mentalities of youth (18–24 years of age) in particular clearly do change, and perhaps keep on changing, as societies become more economically advanced. A *World Youth Survey,* covering eight more-advanced societies (including the United States) and three less-advanced, showed at least two great differences: In the more-advanced nations there was (1) less contact with the family and (2) more "self-interest" and less "society-minded" orientation.[25]

Changing mentalities, it seems quite likely, affect the conduct of higher education sooner and harder than most other segments of society. But they are elusive to identify when they do occur and difficult to anticipate with accuracy, as the Marxists have discovered, to their regret, with their prophecy of the inevitable rise of "class consciousness" to revolutionary levels. John Maynard Keynes did foresee more emphasis, in the economy, on current gratification ("jam today" instead of always "jam tomorrow")—more personal debt instead of more savings with "compound interest."[26] And David Riesman and associates noted the shift from "inner-directed" to "other-directed" mentalities that have so affected social life.[27] Keynes, in effect, saw nomads in the future; and Riesman saw enclaves. What new mentalities may now be being born, like the "adversary culture" was in the 1960s?[28]

Francis Bacon once wrote that "man" tends to begin with certainties and to end with doubts. So it has been in this effort to indicate future possibilities for higher education in the United States in the medium run.

May I conclude, however, that, among the future possibilities, particularly to be considered are these: (1) What is happening in the realm of new knowledge and in the related area of labor markets. (I once asked Ernest Lawrence when I was chancellor at Berkeley and he was director of the Radiation Laboratory: "What are the most important discoveries in the world of science out there waiting to be made?" He replied: "If I really knew, I would go right out there and make them.") (2) What is happening in the visible racial/ethnic composition and attitudes of student bodies and faculties, and in the less visible underworld of community attachments, of citizenship responsibilities, and of orienting mentalities; and in student and faculty political activism—most highly visible when it arises. Thus we face new knowledge and new attitudes, and a resulting changing climate for higher education.[29] (3) What is the trend in the availability of resources to higher education. (4) Is the heightened battle over merit versus equality, in one form or another, to go on forever?

Each of the above considerations will have differing implications for each of the major segments of higher education and for individual institutions within each segment.

Plato's "wheel of education" is really moving at an ever faster rate in response to new knowledge and new skills, but the road it traverses is getting steeper (accumulating resources), developing more potholes (new mentalities and new modes of behavior on campus), and swerving in direction between merit and equality.

Notes

1. See, for 1860–90, the discussion in Lawrence Veysey, *The Emergence of the American University* (Chicago: University of Chicago Press, 1965). For 1960–80, see Clark Kerr, *The Great Transformation in Higher Education, 1960–80* (Albany: State University of New York Press, 1991).

2. Daniel Bell, "The World and the United States in 2013," *Daedalus* 116, no. 3 (Summer 1987): 27.

3. Howard R. Bowen, *The State of the Nation and the Agenda for Higher Education* (San Francisco: Jossey-Bass, 1982), 101–2. It should be noted, however, that Bowen does not define in any specific way what he means by "a nation of educated people."

4. Minority proportions in the younger age cohorts could be even higher: "Three in ten people under 18 years of age in America are now minority. By 2020 or 2030, about one in two could be minority" (Russell Edgerton, "A Long, Deep View of Minority Achievement: L. Scott Miller on the Data," *American Association for Higher Education Bulletin* 43, no. 8 [April 1991]: 4).

5. In the year 2001, however, women are expected to receive, for the first time, more doctoral degrees than men (Debra E. Gerald and William J. Hussar, *Projections of Education Statistics to 2001: An Update* [Washington, D.C.: U.S. National Center for Education Statistics, 1990], table 30).

6. Kevin Murphy and Finis Welch, "Industrial Change and the Rising Importance of Skill," in *Uneven Tides: Rising Inequality in the 1980s,* ed. Sheldon Danzinger and Peter Gottschalk (Ann Arbor: School of Social Work, University of Michigan, 1991).

7. For a view that "education may become a more important element in determining the career and earnings paths of individuals" in the future than in the past, see Frank S. Levy and Richard C. Michel, *The Economic Future of American Families* (Washington, D.C.: Urban Institute Press, 1991), 109.

8. The current official estimate of enrollments in 2001 is 15.9 million, as compared with 13.6 million in fall 1991 (William J. Hussar, *Pocket Projections: Projections of Education Statistics to 2002* [Washington, D.C.: National Center for Education Statistics, 1992], 3).

9. See the discussion in Carnegie Commission on Higher Education, *New Students and New Places* (New York: McGraw-Hill, 1971), 67–71.

10. For a discussion of the decline in Liberal Arts II colleges, see David W. Breneman, "Are We Losing Our Liberal Arts Colleges?" *College Board Review,* no. 156 (Summer 1990): 16–21ff.

11. ECS Task Force on State Policy and Independent Higher Education (John Ashcroft and Clark Kerr, CoChairs), *The Preservation of Excellence in American Higher Education: The Essential Role of Private Colleges and Universities* (Denver: Education Commission of the States, 1990).

12. Carnegie Commission on Higher Education, *The Fourth Revolution: Instructional Technology in Higher Education* (New York: McGraw–Hill, 1972).

13. Elaine El-Khawas, *Campus Trends, 1990,* Higher Education Panel Report, no. 80 (Washington, D.C.: American Council on Education, 1990), 7. (This is the best estimate we have, but I note that it seems on the high side to me.)

14. Robert Maynard Hutchins, *The Learning Society* (New York: Praeger, 1968), 70.

15. See the discussion by Donna E. Shalala, *Mandate for a New Century: Reshaping the Research University's Role in Social Policy,* Eleventh David Dodds Henry Lecture, University of Illinois at Urbana-Champaign, 31 October 1989 (Urbana-Champaign: Office of the President, University of Illinois at Urbana-Champaign, 1990).

16. See Nell P. Eurich, *Corporate Classrooms: The Learning Business* (Princeton: Carnegie Foundation for the Advancement of Teaching, 1985); and Nell P. Eurich, *The Learning Industry: Education for Adult Workers* (Princeton: Carnegie Foundation for the Advancement of Teaching, 1990).

17. See the discussion in Paul Seabury, ed., *Universities in the Western World* (New York: Free Press, 1970).

18. See the discussion in Ernest L. Boyer, *Scholarship Reconsidered: Priorities of the Professoriate* (Princeton: Carnegie Foundation for the Advancement of Teaching, 1990), of how "service," while given "token recognition," is "consistently underrated" (28).

19. Increasing numbers, particularly of younger faculty members, apparently are avoiding committee assignments or performing them in a perfunctory manner—they take time and they increasingly involve unpleasant hassles and even personal enmities. The phenomenon of the free rider is inherent in the "logic of collective action." In any collective endeavor, there are overhead costs to be borne; some members will bear more of these costs than others, and some may bear no costs at all. This is true in trade unions, bar associations, churches, leagues of women voters, and all other organizations of any appreciable size. Consequently, there can be exploitation, by those who do little or nothing, of those who do more or most. Such exploitation can be particularly costly in academic life organized on the basis of collegiality. If it became epidemic, the foundations of shared governance could be weakened. (See the discussion in Mancur Olson, *The Logic of Collective Action* [Cambridge: Harvard University Press, 1965], 29–35.)

20. Harvard Faculty of Arts and Sciences, *Dean's Report,* 1990–91 (Cambridge: Harvard University), 12.

21. See Carnegie Foundation for the Advancement of Teaching, *The Conditions of the Professoriate: Attitudes and Trends* (Princeton: Carnegie Foundation for the Advancement of Teaching, 1989), which notes that 75 percent of faculty members at research universities rate the sense of community on their campus as "fair" or "poor."

22. For a discussion of "nomadic man," see Jacques Attali, *Millenium* (New York: Random House, 1991).

23. See the discussion in Institute for the Study of Social Change (Troy Duster, Director), *The Diversity Project* (Berkeley: University of California at Berkeley, 1991). The authors also suggest a possible "idealistic" "third experience" of cultural, ethnic, and racial diversity, a stage beyond "zero-sum conflict," in which "people come together across different cultural experiences, and in that coming together produce an experience that is transcendent, greater than the sum of the individual parts" (53).

24. See the discussion in L. A. Kaufman, "Emerging from the Shadows of the 1960s," *Socialist Review* 20, no. 4 (October-December 1990): 11–20. The quotations are from this source.

25. *The Youth of the World and Japan: The findings of the Second World Youth Survey, 1978,* Youth Bureau, Prime Minister's Office of Japan (1978).

26. "Economic Prospects for Our Grandchildren," in John Maynard Keynes, *Essays in Persuasion* (New York: Harcourt-Brace, 1932), 370.

27. David Riesman, *The Lonely Crowd: A Study of the Changing American Character* (New Haven: Yale University Press, 1950). (In collaboration with Reuel Denney and Nathan Glazer.)

28. Lionel Trilling, *Beyond Culture: Essays on Literature and Learning* (New York: Harcourt Brace Jovanovich, 1965), Preface.

29. For the main dangers that Derek Bok sees for the future of universities in the areas of (1) "the politicized university," (2) "the overextended university," and (3) "the commercialized university," see Harvard University, *The President's Report 1989–1990* (Cambridge: Harvard University, 1991).

CHAPTER 2

Challenges to Be Faced:

Advancing the Quality of the Future Performance
of American Higher Education

*Higher education in the United States is now entering a period of ma-
ture development after a prolonged childhood, youth, and young adult-
hood (a period of three hundred years). The times of great and assured
growth are past. A change of life is hard upon higher education, with a
new series of issues—a new list of choices to be made, and some un-
accustomed self-doubts. Even institutions, including those within higher
education and also within religion, having most nearly eternal life can
enter times of uncertainty. This seems to be one such time for colleges
and universities. Thus they need to be aware of what problems they may
face and to consider what corrective measures they might take.*

*The period ahead (roughly defined as the academic faculty generation
of 1990 to 2010) poses some new challenges to higher education decision makers and some old challenges in new forms.*

Management of Stasis in Overall Growth
but with Changes in Programs

For thirty-five decades higher education in the United States has been
practicing addition and multiplication. Student enrollment has gone from 9
students—all at Harvard—in 1640 to 14 million in 1991 in thirty-three hundred institutions, and expenditures from a few hundred British pounds to
$100 billion. Within this pattern of growth, American higher education has
accommodated many changes and taken on many new functions.

Higher education now faces a long-term situation unprecedented in the
past hundred years (1870–1990): It must change and add functions with less
growth in enrollments and financial resources to aid adjustment. It must do
both new things and old things better but within more static parameters of
enrollments and resources. It must manage to be dynamic without so much
addition and multiplication, and it must learn to subtract and divide cre-
atively. The new will be accommodated not so much by growth as, of necessity, by invasion of the old, and this is much more controversial in campus

politics. For example, if there is an explosion in enrollments in some field, as there was earlier in business administration, how will it be handled? What will be cut?

Kenneth Boulding once wrote a most interesting article on the "management of decline" of growth when decline seemed likely in the 1980s and 1990s. Much of his advice applies almost equally to the management of stasis. He said that "we are now entering the age of slowdown"—as the railroads did long ago. He noted in particular:

> Perhaps the crucial problem of the declining sector is that its administration becomes more difficult and the quality of administrators is apt to decline as the able ones find more attractive opportunities in the expanding sectors.
>
> The skills of managing a declining institution are not only different from but are probably in some sense greater than those required to manage institutional growth. There is in the former greater need for empathy and for an all too rare mixture of compassion and realism, and for the creative widening of agendas. The manager of a declining institution is required to think of more things that haven't been thought of. In a growing institution mistakes are easily corrected; in a declining institution they are not.[1]

Higher education has managed fast growth spectacularly well. Now it must manage slow growth, but in a society that relies upon its colleges and universities more and more for its future vitality. Slow growth will be harder to manage so spectacularly. Higher education will need to rely more on internal readjustments instead of external extensions. There will be at least two negative consequences: some likely loss of dynamism, and clearly greater strains on the processes of governance.

While the historical expansionist aspects of higher education—growing enrollments and resources—will recede in importance, societal expectations for the performance of higher education will not. A great advantage of American higher education in world competition has been its comparative dynamism. It is essential that it not be lost or, at least, not diminished too greatly, for there is still much to do.

We have done comparatively well versus most other nations in the past in adjusting the levels of access to higher education to meet social demand, in responding to the labor market, in improving research and development, and in depending on merit in the admission and promotion of students and faculty members at the higher academic levels, and in many other ways. We are doing less well now in each of these areas as we encounter new problems:

> Student access: We are doing less well with underserved minorities than we do with the majority population.

Contributions to the labor market: Some gaps are showing up— much more in primary and secondary than in higher education—in the acquisition of basic skills and knowledge, and in the development of productive work habits.

Research and development: Some other nations, particularly Germany and Japan, are now catching up with us.

Merit: More and more of our professoriate (two-thirds to three-quarters) operates within a system essentially based on seniority, and more and more of our students are judged mostly on meeting minimum standards of performance.

Strengthening Decision-making Processes

Higher education will need to strengthen its decision-making processes in order to remain dynamic. It is not now well set up to make hard decisions. In terms of governance, it is a series of more or less independent "estates" that are loosely coordinated by the presidents,[2] many of whom, like Louis XVI of France, have lost their heads in the course of attempted coordination. A particularly confusing aspect of the estates model is that authority flows upward and downward and sideways in contorted patterns.

I would stress three current imperatives in particular: reversing the decline in the citizenship roles of faculty members; retaining and even increasing presidential and trustee involvement in an advisory capacity in academic affairs—keeping them more at the center of the entire enterprise;[3] and stressing the importance of the mechanisms of "consultation and accountability"[4] —distributing information, getting feedback, building consensus—and spec ifying accountability. The estates model can work well only with consultation and consensus building, with the president as the chief communicator and consensus seeker and not just as head of the administrative bureaucracy.

Higher education will need to find ways to subtract as well as to add, to reduce less-useful areas in order to make way for the more useful, as Duke and Stanford, among others, have done so courageously and judiciously in recent times. There will be some net benefits to quality as older and less-beneficial programs are replaced by newer and more-useful programs, resulting in an improvement in the overall level of performance by doing more of what can be done best. This is much harder to accomplish in times of growth, when necessity does not make it so imperative to eliminate weaker programs.

Tough decision making is subject to the dictates of two "laws," each of which causes difficulties:

Bowen's Law I: "Institutions raise as much money as they can and spend it all." (Howard R. Bowen)[5]

Bowen's Law II: Costs per student in higher education rise at the rate of the economy-wide cost index plus 2 percent over the long run. (William G. Bowen)[6]

Law I means that institutions of higher education do not conserve resources for future use—no "rainy day" funds. Law II means that institutions of higher education need more outside resources all the time to stay even, since it seems that they cannot internally easily, if at all, gain resources from increased productivity, as do many other institutions of society—at historical rates averaging 2 percent a year. And, thus, productivity gains offset cost rises more in the economy as a whole than in higher education. The public wonders why. The answer is simple: Productivity has remained constant. This "law" may need to be reexamined in the period ahead.

Even accepting these two laws, there are ways to make better use of resources, and they need to be cultivated.[7]

Overall, the related requirements of commitment to dynamic change and to provision of tough decision making both conduce toward a more coordinated central decision-making process involving trustees, presidents, and faculty leaders.

Handling Polycentric Conflicts

Internal conflicts have always been endemic in American higher education. In the first two centuries and more (1636–1870), they consisted mostly of student opposition to *in loco parentis* rules—*in loco parentis* mostly won; and of the faculty contest with trustees over who had the ultimate governing authority, as at Harvard and William and Mary—the trustees (Calvinist model) mostly won against the faculty (Anglican model).[8] Then, still later, trustees and presidents became clearly dominant after the War between the States for about forty years (1870–1910), giving rise to the attacks by Thorstein Veblen and Upton Sinclair, among others, and to the organization of the American Association of University Professors. This period was followed by an increasingly accepted truce, as "shared governance" became the standard model (1910–60).[9] The 1960s then saw the student revolts, and the 1970s and 1980s the restoration of faculty authority, including, in some places, via unionization. Now we enter the 1990s.

Now there are more conflicts of students versus students and faculty members versus faculty members, and of some of each with administrators and trustees.[10] These are over both ends and means. Both the issues and the means of their advancement are more subject to debate. Earlier bipolar conflicts are being replaced by polycentric conflicts.

Polycentric conflicts require more knowledge of what is going on—more presidents who walk the campus, more deans of students (once deans of student deportment and now deans of student advising) who have sensitive antennae constantly alert, and more provosts who work the faculty clubs and the dinner parties. Polycentric conflicts also require better means of consultation and advice between the administration and the faculty, including through elected faculty councils that meet regularly with the presidents and easy recourse to ballots to ascertain across-the-board faculty opinions rather than those of activist minorities alone.[11] They also require a better flow of information to faculties about new developments and new policies.

The new environment additionally requires better codes governing political conduct on campus and better means of independent judicial enforcement. It must be accepted by now that most faculties will not discipline students and fellow faculty members for actions in the political arena, and that it is both difficult and unwise for the administration to serve in the roles of both prosecutor and judge. Consequently, some independent tribunal needs to be established, probably appointed by the trustees after advice from the faculty council and the president. It is probably also prudent to externalize conflict as much as possible by the use of the external law, external police, and external courts.[12] Academic communities do not handle these matters well—they are too often unwilling to temper mercy with justice, and these matters are very divisive within each campus community. Additionally, highly capable lawyers and public relations experts (including those with expertise on how to handle TV) are more urgently needed.

In the choice of presidents, it is important to select individuals who are willing and able to endure conflict situations that require resiliency and the ability to act under pressure, and who have the patience and the inventiveness to engage constructively in agreement building. Presidents now need to understand passions as well as interests. The older interests were easier to handle (one claim for more resources or preferment versus another), for they responded to cost-benefit analysis and to compromise. The passions are likely to be inflamed, not reduced, by the assessment of costs, and their owners to be contemptuous of compromise. It is now more a world of all-or-none and now-or-never instead of a world of more-or-less and now-or-next-time, and of high-minded convictions versus low-minded calculations.

Hirschman has written, in relation to history, "contrasting the favorable effects that follow when men are guided by their interests with the calamitous state of affairs that prevails when men give free rein to their passions."[13] "Heroic passions" can lead to "coercion and repression"; the pursuit of "interests" is more likely to involve persuasion and conciliation. They represent the diverse worlds of the fanatic and of the pragmatist, of victory-or-defeat and of compromise, of intolerance and of tolerance. The academic world has known passions (as during the religious wars in Europe) and interests (as in the period of shared governance in the United States). Now it is coming to know both.

What might be called the Hirschman scenario of the rise of passions on campus, as compared with the concentration on interests, is a possible scenario but not a certainty. It did play a significant role in the 1960s, and some of the present and advancing issues of the 1990s create a stage for a potential revival. However, the central theme of higher education has been, and very well may continue to be, an emphasis on cognitive behavior, including careful analysis based on facts. On the other hand, I have observed occasionally how faculty members who are coldly analytical in their areas of specialization can be hotly emotional outside them about political and social issues—how they can verify facts religiously within their specialities and react wildly to unchecked rumors outside them. Also, some students have not been committed to a culture of objectivity. The Hirschman scenario must be accepted as endemic within the groves of academe, and occasionally reaches epidemic proportions. When it does, it affects the choice and conduct of presidents and other academic leaders.

Advancing Community Welfare and Citizenship Responsibilities

As the sense of allegiance to the academic community grows weaker and the attachment to personal advancement (even including exploitative practices) among faculty members grows stronger, the campus needs to take counteractive measures.[14] These measures start with selecting faculty members with some attention to their good citizenship records in prior endeavors—as college students and in earlier employment, as shown by participation in leadership roles on campus and service roles off-campus. Also, "the faculty reward structure system needs to be modified to recognize the importance of committing time to the governing process"[15] in considering promotions and in distributing recognition—for example, an "outstanding citizenship" award to parallel "outstanding teacher" awards. Additionally, faculty members can be drawn into good citizenship the more they are informed about developments on campus, the more they are consulted, and the more they are involved in making decisions.

Facilities can help: The campus can assist with the provision of housing in the vicinity of the campus, attractive cultural programs, active faculty clubs, and coffee lounges for faculty members in each major academic building. Departmental size is very important. Beyond some modest size, there seems to be at work a law of declining involvement with growing numbers as senior faculty members know less well their junior colleagues and are less inclined to help and advise them, and as some senior members withdraw into isolation even from their fellow senior colleagues. My observation is that there is a sharp drop of involvement in departments of more than thirty members and often a collapse where there are sixty or more.

Administrators can serve as models by serving on faculty committees, thus recognizing their importance. For example, the president and/or provost can participate, ex officio, in all committees considering tenure appointments (as historically they do at Harvard) and in all educational policy committees, and with this experience with the quality of the service of individual faculty members, these officers are better able to have it taken into account in the reward process.

Explicit codes of conduct can serve as guides to faculty members and as bases for enforcement action, through an impartial judicial procedure, for grave dereliction of responsibilities.

Shared governance was won in hard battles. It has proved its great value. Now it appears to be of declining effectiveness, not due to the actions of presidents or trustees but by increasing faculty default. Should this process continue, it is almost inevitable that administrators will gradually fill in the gaps—particularly department chairs and deans. This will make more important their careful selection, the constant review of their performance, and a system of more enticing rewards. It also probably means longer terms of service for those who perform well in maintaining and improving the quality of their faculties.[16] It also probably means more reliance on high-level departmental administrators to handle business affairs in departments of substantial size.

Some departments retreat from controversy, with more reliance on seniority alone in personnel decisions once an appointment has been made. Some decide to hire entirely or mostly at the tenure level, thus having more and better information to rely on in making appointment decisions than if they were made at the instructor or assistant professor level, and avoiding controversies thereafter—including over "open files," by following a policy of advancement on the basis of seniority.

Effective governance must go on, even if the duty of effective participation is not fully shared by all faculty members as a part of their implicit contract of mutual obligations that explicitly includes tenure as the other side of the bargain.

Maintaining Leadership in the Intellectual World

In the course of the twentieth century the United States has established clear leadership in the world of science and scholarship. This is evidenced by the award of the highest scientific honors (table 1) and by dominance in journal articles and citations (table 2). In some twenty-five hundred leading journals in fields of science, one-third of all articles have been written by Americans and one-half of all citations are to contributions made by Americans, although the United States has only 5 percent of the world population.

TABLE 1

Academic Awards by Nation

Country	Nobel Prizes	Fields Medals	Total
United States	53	18	71
United Kingdom	7	4	11
France	3	6	9
West Germany	10		10
Sweden	4	1	5
Italy	2	1	3
Japan	2	1	3
USSR		3	3
Switzerland	2		2
Argentina	1		1
Canada	2		2
Denmark	1		1
Netherlands	1		1
Norway	1		1

Nobel Prizes awarded through 1990 in physics, chemistry, physiology/medicine, and economics. Nation of citizenship of winners: Some bear dual citizenship and are counted twice.

Fields Medals in mathematics awarded through 1990. Nation of institutional affiliation at time of award.

TABLE 2

Articles and Citations in 2,649 Journals by National Source:
All Science Fields Combined

National source	World Share (%)		Citations
	Articles (1)	Citations (2)[a]	Ratio: Articles (3)[b]
United States	36.81	50.82	1.38
United Kingdom	8.96	9.61	1.07
Netherlands	1.70	1.93	1.14
Sweden	1.64	1.94	1.18
Switzerland	1.22	1.79	1.47
Denmark	0.82	0.92	1.13

Sources: Columns (1) and (2) are taken from A. Shubert, N. Glänzer, and T. Braun, "Scientometric Data Files," *Scientometrics* 16 (June 1989): 218. Column (3) is calculated from (1) and (2).

[a]In terms of percentage of total citations, Japan and Germany each had 5.8% of the total, but they fell below 1.00 in column 3.
[b]All other nations fell below 1.00.

The ratio of number of citations to number of articles is a crude index of quality—it suggests that the contributions cited are those most valued by other scholars in the field. Only Switzerland has a higher ratio than the United States.

Status as the world center of higher learning has shifted over history from Greece in the classical age, to the Muslim world in the Middle Ages, then successively to Italy (1540–1610), England (1660–1730), France (1770–1830), Germany (1810–1920), and the United States (1920–90).[17] The pattern since 1540 has been for leadership to last an average of eighty years. "If this pattern holds true for the U.S.A., then its scientific prosperity, which began in 1920, will end in 2000."[18] But this is sheer speculation based on a small number of observations of national histories and with no persuasive explanation of why eighty years should be the pattern. However, it is somewhat ominous that the origin of U.S. patents has been shifting away from American sources, and that both Germany and Japan are rising as centers of patents.[19]

To remain the single leading center, the United States needs to retain its highly competitive system of higher education among institutions and place highest emphasis on merit in the selection of students and faculty members, particularly in the (150) Liberal Arts I colleges and the (100) Research Universities, (in the Carnegie classification) which produce and employ most of the leading scientists within higher education. These 250 institutions are on the front lines. Also, it would be helpful if the federal government would concentrate more of its research and development (R&D) funds on the universities. The percentage in 1989 of R&D performed by U.S. higher education institutions was 14 percent (only the United Kingdom's was lower), but all other advanced industrial countries generally have higher proportions.[20]

Earning Autonomy and Resources and Freedom

Not the Bible, not the Constitution, not any inalienable rights confer autonomy and resources and freedom on institutions of higher education. However each of the three may have been achieved in the course of history, their continuation at high levels is earned by conduct.

Autonomy in the United States has been, and is, at a high comparative level. Institutional governance via trustees, presidents, and faculty senates has generally been at an advanced level of competence and has gained respect. This respect may now be eroding marginally, mostly due to costs rising above the general level of inflation and to rising doubts about the integrity of conduct by institutions and faculty members. Both of these areas deserve careful attention.

Resources devoted to higher education have also been maintained at a generous level. Sustaining this level has now become less assured, particularly as new economic resources are becoming available at a reduced rate and as other social needs continue to rise in competition for them. Higher education can earn additional resources as it demonstrates their efficient and effective use and shows sensitivity to expanding areas of social needs, such as these:

- A more intensive talent hunt among minorities, women, and low-income families.[21]
- More remedial assistance to students admitted on the basis of "affirmative action" to offset prior deficits. The real test is graduation, not admission.
- More attention to the needs of older students through reentry and extension programs.
- More attention to the interests of the total population and particularly to the cultural interests of the whole community, to the need for special advice and service to all post-high-school youth and not just those who select college, and to the quality of locally available health services, as through area health education centers.[22]
- More assistance to the high schools.
- More responsiveness to the need for improvement in "general education" programs.
- More attention to the transmission of research results into early and effective application.
- More commitment to the long-run development of a "nation of educated people."

The original land-grant idea was service to all elements of the population. The population was then largely rural; now it is largely urban, which has important implications. Institutions of higher education should never forget that taxes are paid by everybody. The College of Agriculture is still an important model.

Academic freedom has now been largely won from the state, the courts, the church, the trustees. Now it must be preserved internally from willful minorities that do not respect the rights of others and who believe that they alone have the correct opinions. The battles against the Right on the outside have been concluded with victories. Now the battles are with the Left and with special interest groups on the inside, and they are more frequently being lost. The earlier battles unified the campus against the external enemy; the newer battles divide it. The earlier battles were largely impersonal; the newer battles are intensely personal.

Advancing Equality and Merit

The polity requires greater equality, the economy greater merit. The two, which are not absolute opposites, are, however, to a degree, in conflict. The task is to make them as compatible and as reinforcing as possible. The best policy is an aggressive program of compensatory equality of opportunity. This results in the maximum discovery and advancement of talent. It calls for the greatest educational resources directed to those with the most deprivation at the earlier levels of education and to those with the greatest proven ability at the later levels. These efforts are best served by some differentiation of functions among institutions—some more devoted to discovering and motivating talent, and others more to its advancement once discovered and motivated. There is no perfect solution, but some solutions are much better than others.[23]

The above challenges, among others, lead to the conclusion that a "time of troubles" lies ahead.

Notes

1. Kenneth E. Boulding, "The Management of Decline," *AGB Reports* 17, no. 5 (September-October 1975): 4–9. Quoted with permission of the Association of Governing Boards of Universities and Colleges.

2. For a discussion of the "estates model" of governance, see Clark Kerr, *The Great Transformation of Higher Education, 1960–1980* (Albany: State University of New York Press, 1991), Introduction to part 3. The estates model is different from that of a loosely-coupled system in that it emphasizes that each estate has a different model of government: collegial for faculty, bureaucratic for administration, market for student choices, political for relations with external interests—although there is loose coupling among the estates. (See Karl Weick, "Educational Organizations as Loosely Coupled Systems," in *The Dynamics of Organizational Change*, ed. J. Victor Baldridge and Terence Deal [Berkeley: McCutcheon, 1983], chap. 2.)

3. For example, by exercising the right of presidents and trustees to be informed about academic developments and by using the privilege of commenting on such reports. For this and other problems at the president-trustee level, see National Commission on Strengthening Presidential Leadership (Clark Kerr, Chair), *Presidents Make a Difference* (Washington, D.C.: Association of Governing Boards of Universities & Colleges, 1984); Clark Kerr and Marian L. Gade, *The Many Lives of Academic Presidents: Time, Place, and Character* (Washington, D.C.: Association of Governing Boards of Universities & Colleges, 1986); and Clark Kerr and Marian L. Gade, *The Guardians: Boards of Trustees of American Colleges and Universities* (Washington, D.C.: Association of Governing Boards of Universities & Colleges, 1989).

4. See the excellent discussion of "the seventh principle" by Henry Rosovsky, *The University: An Owner's Manual* (New York: Norton, 1990), chap. 15. He identifies this principle as the "most important."

5. Howard R. Bowen, "Financial Needs of the Campus," in *The Corporation and the Campus: Corporate Support of Higher Education in the 1970's* (New York: Academy of Political Science, 1970), 81. See also the discussion in Henry M. Levin, "Raising Productivity in Higher Education," *Journal of Higher Education* 62, no. 3 (May–June 1991): 241–62. Levin notes that higher education is "labor intensive," and that "there are technical limits to finding ways of reducing labor costs," and that the "decentralized levels of the organization and the lack of incentive" also impede efforts to reduce costs—the levels where costs are mostly set are far removed from direct control with pressures to reduce costs and are buffered against these pressures.

6. See the discussion in William G. Bowen, *The Economics of the Major Private Universities* (Berkeley: Carnegie Commission on Higher Education, 1968), 22, 23.

7. See the discussion in Howard R. Bowen (with Gordon Douglass), *Efficiency in Liberal Education* (New York: McGraw-Hill, 1971); Howard R. Bowen, *The Costs of Higher Education* (San Francisco: Jossey-Bass, 1980); and Carnegie Commission on Higher Education, *The More Effective Use of Resources* (New York: McGraw-Hill, 1972).

8. See the discussion by Walter P. Metzger in "Academic Governance: An Evolutionary Perspective," in *Governing Tomorrow's Campus*, ed. Jack H. Schuster and Lynn H. Miller (New York: Macmillan, 1989).

9. See the AAUP policy statements, in Louis Joughin, ed., *Academic Freedom and Tenure: A Handbook of the American Association of University Professors* (Madison: University of Wisconsin Press, 1969).

10. For a discussion of the fractionalization of students (and faculties) into "enclaves," see Institute for the Study of Social Change (Troy Duster, Director), *The Diversity Project* (Berkeley: University of California at Berkeley, 1991). Also, Levine has noted "the most pressing need today is for each campus to define clearly what it means by diversity and to develop a long-term, comprehensive plan for achieving that definition" (Arthur Levine, "The Meaning of Diversity," *Change* 23, no. 5 [September–October 1991]: 5).

11. This is said from the point of view of holding the campus together. The view of political activists can be quite different. John H. Schaar, for example, argues for "All Power to the Fragments" and adds that "it is a rock-bottom part of our condition that if opinions are consulted and votes counted, there will be no radical change" (John H. Schaar, *Legitimacy in the Modern State* [New Brunswick, N.J.: Transaction Books, 1981], 307, 308).

12. I once considered this treason against institutional autonomy and a cowardly way out. Now it seems to me to be a shrewd adjustment to new realities—but still personally repugnant.

13. Albert O. Hirschman, *The Passions and the Interests* (Princeton: Princeton University Press, 1977), 32.

14. For a discussion of the general importance of "the concerned citizen" and tendencies for erosion of this role in the United States at large, see Robert N. Bellah

and Associates, *Habits of the Heart* (New York: Harper & Row, 1985). It is difficult to develop the "concerned citizen" in a world where it is increasingly possible for "people to work together without being together in one place." (See the discussion in Charles Handy, *The Age of Unreason* [Cambridge: Harvard Business School Press, 1989].) A professor in one continent may be more in touch with his or her "fax pal" across the country or world than with the colleague next door or spouse at work across town.

15. See the discussion in Jack H. Schuster, "Governance and the Changing Faculty Condition," in *Governing Tomorrow's Campus.*

16. Here again I have changed my views. I once favored shorter terms in order to remove some old-line authoritarian German-type chairs and to obtain new energy, and so acted as chancellor at Berkeley and later as president of the University of California. This was when I thought that all faculty members should be willingly prepared to serve as department chairs as part of their normal citizenship responsibilities, and most were; and that all faculty members, as a matter of course, took seriously their shared governance responsibilities, and most did.

17. For the period beginning with 1540, see Yuasa Mitsutomo, "The Shifting Center of Scientific Activity in the West: From the Sixteenth to the Twentieth Century," in *Science and Society in Modern Japan: Selected Historical Sources,* ed. Shigeru Nakayama, David L. Swain, and Eri Yagi (Cambridge: MIT Press, 1974); also published in *Japanese Studies in the History of Science,* no. 1 (1962): 57–75.

18. Mitsutomo, "The Shifting Center," 84.

19. Patenting by Americans declined over the decade 1972 to 1983, and then rose again (51,500 in 1972; 33,000 in 1983; 40,500 in 1988). In the 1980s, foreign patenting in the United States was rising at a much faster rate than U.S. domestic patenting (other countries: 24,500 in 1980 and 37,500 in 1988). The Japanese rate more than doubled: 7,100 in 1980 and 16,100 in 1988. The German rate increased by about 30 percent—from 5,700 to 7,300. (National Science Board, *Science and Engineering Indicators—1989,* NSB 89-1, 356; U.S. Department of Commerce, National Technical Information Service, *Industrial Patent Activity in the United States,* part 1 [Washington, D.C., July 1989], A2.)

20. Including Japan at 20.5 percent (*UNESCO Statistical Yearbook* [1990], table 5-11, "R&D Expenditures by Sector of Performance").

21. This would be greatly aided by changes in federal policies toward student aid. They have resulted too much in reducing the burden on middle- and upper-income families and too little in drawing in new students from less advantaged elements of the population. Most grant awards now go to students who would have attended college anyway (Charles F. Manski and David A. Wise, *College Choice in America* [Cambridge: Harvard University Press, 1983], 23), and this is even more true for subsidized loans.

22. See the discussion in Charles E. Odegaard, *Area Health Education Centers: The Pioneering Years, 1972–1978* (Berkeley: Carnegie Council on Policy Studies in

Higher Education, 1979); and see Malcolm Watts, M.D., and Clark Jones, *The Story of the California AHEC System: California Area Health Education Centers: 1972– 1989* (Fresno: California AHEC System, 1990); and Clark Kerr, "After Twenty Years," *The National AHEC Bulletin* 8, no. 3 (Winter 1990).

23. Those who would give up on merit altogether should reread John Rawls's difference principle. This "principle would allocate resources in education, say, so as to improve the long-term expectation of the least favored. If this end is attained by giving more attention to the better endowed, it is permissible; otherwise not" (John Rawls, *A Theory of Justice* [Cambridge: Harvard University Press, 1971], 101).

CHAPTER 3

New Focus on Leadership

There are times and places when and where it can be said, with good reasons, that a college does not really need a president.[1] The 1990s will not be such a time except in the most unusual of circumstances. There are too many urgent assignments for leadership. The general theme in this chapter is that leadership will be both more necessary and more difficult. It must, under current circumstances, be based less on power and more on persuasion. Even more than in the past, the leaders of the future will need to be like the legendary Proteus, who both "knows all things, and has the power of assuming different shapes in order to escape being questioned."

This chapter is a combination of three related speeches on this theme. The first of these speeches was given to the Twenty-ninth Annual Meeting of the American Association of State Colleges and Universities in San Francisco in November 1989.[2] Mostly it was attended by presidents of institutions. I was telling them, but I am not sure that they agreed, that they had been going through an easy decade in the 1980s. They seemed more in agreement, however, that the next decade would hold more difficulties for presidents and that they should be prepared for them or, by implication, seek an early exit. The greater the problems, the greater the testing of governance mechanisms, and the more likely it is, particularly, that "presidents make a difference." Everybody behaves more or less alike at a cocktail party (the 1980s), but not on the firing lines (the 1990s).

The second speech was addressed to presidents at a "presidents only" session of the American Council on Education meeting in San Francisco in January 1991.[3] Judging by the discussion, presidents entering the 1990s were more concerned than I have ever seen them before with (1) how long might they expect to continue in office, (2) what sort of positions might they hold after the presidency, and (3) whether the presidency, as a segment of their lives, will have been worth it in retrospect. Mostly, however, they appeared, as presidents before them, to look forward to meeting the challenges ahead—those who do not so anticipate problems to solve seldom accept presidencies or seldom make much of a mark if they do. The presidency is not for the risk-aversive.

The third speech was at a meeting centered around the problems of "shared governance," whether that shared governance was via the traditional AAUP model or via unionization. It was attended by a mixture of presidents, faculty council and union leaders, and academic experts in the field.[4] The questions and discussions that followed my presentation served to confirm to me that shared governance is in trouble on many and perhaps most campuses, and at an unfortunate time in history—unfortunate because there is so much to do together: recruit new faculty members, reconsider the undergraduate curriculum, adjust to the new composition of student bodies. After seventy years of advances in shared governance (1920–90), it now looks as if a period of retrogression may have started, as more faculty members are more reluctant to engage in the tasks of shared governance. But then trustee governance may also be in trouble, particularly in large systems, as trustees became farther removed from campus life; and presidential governance, too, as presidents are more "boxed in" by other elements of governing structures.

All three of the meetings confirmed me in my view that there are new pressures on leadership.

There are many problems, but it is, as yet at least, extreme to say that, now that universities and colleges have run out of "labor negotiators" as presidents, they "may have to draw on retired Mafia chiefs."[5]

Some historical periods create more vulnerabilities than others for leadership, and particularly for presidential leadership. Contexts are more difficult; decisions have more dangerous possibilities. The 1990s appear, in advance, to be such a period of vulnerabilities.

Every president faces the possibility of an F grade on some important examination. The grading system is an unusual one: Nine A's and one F average out to an F.[6] Any major recent failure (for example, failure to have examined carefully the accounting system for federal contract overhead) can wipe out (at least temporarily) all the prior record. This may occur even when someone else down the line really took the examination for the president! As a consequence, presidents facing the future should ask not only, What are my opportunities? but also, What are my potential vulnerabilities?

The Board and the President

I should like to address two topics: (1) How the prospective future of American higher education, particularly in the 1990s, may not be like that of the 1980s, and how this next period may test the governance of colleges and universities more severely than in recent years; and (2) how the condition in which board and presidential governance enters this period, is, I believe, from an historical point of view, in a weakened position.

I shall draw, in particular, on observations resulting from three studies made under the auspices of the Association of Governing Boards.[7] These studies involved closer contact with the reality of ongoing governance in academic institutions than any other studies ever made. Altogether, there were more than one thousand interviews in nearly every state in the nation and in every major category of general purpose institutions. In addition, there were fifteen hundred completed questionnaires in a nationwide survey of trustee effectiveness. I know of no similar study so intensive in other fields of organizational leadership—not on corporations, not on trade unions, not on churches, not on political agencies.

Recent and current college and university presidents have been the fortunate ones. History has favored them. The 1980s were one of the easiest of times to be an academic leader. Only two other decades in the twentieth century can match the one just past in this respect—the first (1900–1910) and the third (1920–30). The first decade saw the final triumphant emergence of the American research university, and the early rise to dominance of the United States as the world's most advanced economy. The third decade was one of "return to normalcy" after a war we had helped to win and of normalcy for higher education too. The other decades of this century up to now were variously marked by wars, by depressions, by preparations for the "tidal wave" of students, by student revolts—except for the decade of the 1980s.

Let me contrast the 1980s with the prior two decades. Enrollments held comparatively even, instead of expanding four times over. There were no great student revolts. There were no OPEC oil crises. The great expansion of the community colleges had already taken place, as had the great transformation of four-year state institutions with restricted missions into the multipurpose comprehensive colleges and universities of today. There were no years like 1967–69. In the fall of 1969, any president of an Association of American Universities institution who had served two years was already halfway up the seniority list. In the fall of 1989, on the contrary, it took seven years of service to be halfway up the same list. In 1899, the figure had been eleven. The figure for 1991 is ominous: five years.

The 1990s will not be the worst of years following on the heels of the best of years, but they seem likely to hold some difficulties. Let me quickly note, however, how uncertain it is to predict the future of higher education. We badly missed on three of the four greatest developments of the past thirty years. We did see the "tidal wave" coming, but not the student revolts and not the OPEC crises. Nor did we see that what was billed in advance as the greatest demographic tragedy of all times would be a no-show. But past experience does demonstrate that each succeeding decade develops its own special history, and so, also, will the 1990s.

I see no great overwhelming sudden crisis ahead, but I do see the gradual arrival of more difficult times for many institutions of higher education than in the 1980s. These difficulties are likely to emerge not only slowly but also to different degrees in different types of institutions, but I expect that your counterparts as presidents in 1999 will have had a less relaxed decade than most of you who are here today have had in the past ten years. They, in 1999, like your predecessors in 1969, will be even more conscious than you mostly are today of the harsh fact that grievances accumulate faster against executives in a period of conflicts. Recent history in 1999 is likely to have been written by social tensions in our society and by economic crises more than in 1989, and our institutions of higher education are more likely to have been heavily involved in these tensions and crises. I say this as one who, over the years, has been one of the greatest of optimists about the future of higher education in America.

Relations between boards and presidents have been in the past, and will be in the future, greatly affected by the context in which they take place. Just as easier times mean easier relations, so also more difficult times mean more difficult relations—this has always been true.

How good are the relations today, and what might be done to improve them?

To begin with, the basic governance system of American higher education is, I believe, the best in the world—with great responsibility placed with independent boards of trustees, with comparatively strong presidencies, and with shared governance in academic areas with the faculties. In practice, by and large the system works well, but also, by and large, it can be improved upon.

Overall, we found board/president relations to be in some degree of trouble in about one-fourth of the situations in which we came in contact, in excellent condition in another one-fourth, and in relatively good health in the other half. The most difficult specific situations for presidents, we found, were those where

- the board was internally fractionated;
- the faculty union had direct access to the board, and especially where it controlled it;
- the president was selected and/or evaluated under sunshine (open meeting) procedures;
- a "flagship" institution felt insecure within a larger system.

Problems

But we found some general problems, too, and made many recommendations about them. In particular, I note the following common needs as we confront the 1990s:

Clarification of the respective roles of the board and of the president.

Concentration of both board and president more on long-range issues and less on short-term details.

Advance consideration of the mechanisms, the policies, and the staff competence to handle emergency situations—including elected faculty executive committees with which presidents can consult on a regular basis, and provisions for secret ballots to all faculty members in taking important positions affecting the welfare of the institution rather than at mass meetings with some faculty "enclaves" more represented than others.

More careful board attention to the selection and the care of the president. Board and faculty committees need to go out aggressively to find and recruit able people and not just settle for the last person not to be rejected from among those who have made themselves available.

More board understanding of and sensitivity to the very difficult and important aspects of the relations of the presidential spouse to the institution.

Closer connection of trustees in large systems with the life of the campus, particularly via local boards with substantial authority to make decisions. So many systemwide trustees are now far removed from daily reality.

Personal contact of the president with each trustee, and careful consideration of the quality of the agenda for each meeting.

Protection of the autonomy of the institution and the capacity for effective decision making by boards and presidents. The one phrase of an interviewee that most stays in my mind is this: "The corrals are getting smaller and the barbed wire around them is getting higher."

This leads to my central question: If the surrounding context becomes more difficult, will the by-now more constrained central mechanism for decision making by the board and president be as generally adequate to the task as it has been historically? The answer remains to be given.

After all those interviews, after all those campus visits, after all the reading of history, I have been left with an impression of two great uncertainties in campus governance:

The changing social and economic context of the nation—externally.

The developing relationships, campus by campus, of three sets of personalities—the board, the president/spouse, and faculty leaders—internally. By contrast, the great constant is the nonacademic staff.

We found no "interchangeable light bulbs," as James March once claimed,[8] among presidents—nor among spouses, board members, or faculty leaders; rather, infinite and fascinating variety. All those sensitivities, all those individualities! I started out wondering why presidential terms were so short and getting shorter, and ended up wondering why, given the often stressful circumstances, they sometimes lasted so long. And I came to respect even more the values of loyalty, sense of duty, devotion, and good citizenship—where and to the extent they exist, and particularly within faculties and among staff members.

Be that as it may, the 1990s are here, and if they are a greater time of testing, then the quality of boards, of presidents and their spouses, of faculty leaders, and of their interrelationships at the center of the governing process will also be tested all the more. Thus we need always improving understanding of the roles and the conduct of boards, presidents and spouses, and faculty leaders separately and working together.

The "uses of the past" are not to predict precisely the future—for that is not possible—but to help leaders to be conscious of the need to prepare for all of the best that is possible but also for some of the worst that may be inevitable, to free themselves of "grandiose hopes as of petty concerns," and to remember that many people can profit by, but might also suffer from, the "history their leaders" will help in making for them.[9]

President

Who is the "president" that we are talking about? There are at least three major models of the president circulating in the academic world today. Which model is chosen is basic to any discussion of the changing role of the president.

Models of the Presidency

One model is the "organized anarchy" model, which holds that the presidency is mostly important only to the president: "The college president is an executive who does not know exactly what he should be doing and does not have much confidence that he can do anything important anyway." The president, does, it is conceded, make the "bureaucracy work," but this is not considered to be much of a role.[10]

A second model I shall call the "faculty opinion" model. According to this model, most presidents (over two-thirds) are viewed as "autocratic," which the dictionary defines as "despotic"; and most presidents (nearly two-thirds) are also rated by faculty as "fair" or "poor" in their performances[11]— which implies that they are not very good autocrats or despots. This model is the mirror image of the first. In the first model, the president has only "modest control over the events of college life"; in the second, the president is an autocrat attempting to exercise excessive control. In the first model, presidents "vary within limited ranges";[12] in the second, they vary widely from being autocratic to being democratic—from only one person having a vote to "one person–one vote" among many persons.

The third model I shall call the "presidents make a difference" model.[13] Here the president has more responsibility than any other single person for holding the organization together internally, for defending and advancing it externally, and for selecting or assisting movement in new directions. Presidents vary enormously in their characteristics. The contexts in which they operate also vary enormously and change from time to time, and contexts are as important as the presidents who operate within them—and both must be understood in relation to each other. Mostly, using this model, presidents are rated "good" to "excellent" within their contexts.

Take your pick.[14] My pick is the third model. I consider both of the others to be too simplistic and also wrong as basic models, although each does fit some specific situations. The first is too negative about the presidency, the second about actual presidents. Most places and most times "presidents make a difference," and for the better. In the late 1960s, however, many presidents were puppets with powerful events pulling the strings that determined how they behaved—"performance is largely an act of God or at least not clearly under the control of the president," as Jim March observed.[15] In still earlier times, there were some "Captains of Erudition," to use the phrase of Thorstein Veblen,[16] but they have, contrary to some continuing faculty perceptions, mostly gone the way of the dodo bird or are at least an endangered species. Both mere puppets and bold captains are now rare cases

I raise the issue of models because the model chosen is essential to any discussion of changing roles of the president. In the organized-anarchy model, the president is a passive force—more acted upon than acting—and thus the role is not an important one, and changes in it also are not important. In the faculty-opinion model, the president is more likely to be a negative than a positive force in the solution of current challenges, and so the lesser the role, the better. In the presidents-make-a-difference model, the president is a key player, and usually *the* key player, and so how he or she plays this role is very important—within the context.

The first model concentrates on the royalty and bureaucracy functions of the presidency; the second on the quality (or absence thereof) of micromanagement; and the third on general leadership. In all models, there is, of course, also some "garbage" to handle.[17]

The model chosen affects the approach to the choice of a president. In the first model, this is a not very important decision (presidents have little influence and are mostly all alike anyway). And it is better to get someone more interested in the consumption than in the production aspects of the position, and who knows in advance that he or she cannot be a hero and will only cause trouble by trying to be one.

In the second model, one should look for a person who does not seek to be any more influential than anyone else (one person among many)—the president as "servant";[18] and the search committee should expect to fail two out of three times even in this modest assignment and get an autocrat instead, and also end up with someone who is judged "fair" or "poor" however they approach their role. The choice and evaluation of the president is often the biggest single game on campus. Were the persons chosen such disappointments, as the faculty-opinion model suggests, it would be a sad commentary on the choice process in which faculty representatives play such a significant part—they usually, at a minimum, have veto power to eliminate any person from the final list for choice. Who then is most responsible if two out of three presidents are judged "fair" to "poor"?

The third model says that the presidency is the most important single position on campus, and that all that effort that goes into the choice of a president mostly is worth it—most persons chosen are from among the best of those with prior success in earlier positions, and most are also judged effective, once chosen, for at least a modest period of office.

This model, which I shall be using, also places a high emphasis on the context of the presidency as well as on the person of the president, and so I shall be addressing mostly the changing contexts of the presidency—first, the long-range changes, and, second, possibilities for the 1990s. I shall also comment on how the changing long-run and contemporary contexts might affect the conduct of presidents—how they might wish to approach their positions.

A Digression on John W. Gardner

First, however, I should like to digress on the views of John W. Gardner. He recently published the book *On Leadership*.[19] He himself has been a leader, and has seen many leaders at work, as head of the Carnegie Corporation, as secretary of health, education, and welfare, as founder of the National Coalition, of Common Cause, and of the Independent Sector, and as a director of several large corporations. His concern in his new book is with leadership in general; ours is with the special case of leadership in higher education. His view of leadership at large is consistent with the presidents-make-a-difference model of the college and university presidency. According to Gardner:

Leaders have essential roles in helping to choose goals, in asserting values, in motivating others, in managing the enterprise, in seeking unity, in representing the enterprise externally, in advancing renewal, in using and influencing the use of power.

Followers are important too. They are not just passive; there are conflicts among them, and they change in their composition.

There are many kinds of leaders.

There are many kinds of followers.

There are many diverse settings.

The historical trends have been toward larger scale organizations—and this puts more emphasis on "leadership teams"; toward fractionalization of constituencies—and this puts more emphasis on consensus-building; toward "multiple colliding systems"—"the war of the parts against the whole is the current problem of pluralism today"; and toward a new "anti-leadership vaccine" across the land.

In sum, leadership is both becoming more important (we "cry out for leadership") and getting more difficult. So also in higher education.

I shall next turn to some generalizations about the trends I see, but I start with the caveat that no generalizations about higher education are true except this one: No generalization about higher education is true, since each campus has its own heritage, its own setting, its own course of future development. Now for some other generalizations.

Long-run Trends in the Governance of Higher Education

Colleges and universities have become much larger and much more complex institutions. As late as 1800, Harvard had one president, three professors, and four tutors.

Power and influence have shifted very substantially. More of each is now in external hands—in state coordinating councils, in federal agencies, in the courts. In one area, however, that of external "interests," there has been a countertendency as agricultural organizations, for example, have lost control over colleges of agriculture, and local medical associations, as another example, over schools of medicine.[20] As one consequence of generally intensified external controls and influences, staff members have increased greatly in numbers and in influence in the areas of public relations and legal services.

Power has also shifted in other ways internally. The big gainers have been the faculties and the student market. The losers have been the boards of trustees and the presidents—boards more than the presidents, as boards are now more dependent on presidents to inform them and to carry out their wishes as institutions have become larger and more complex.

The presidency has changed. It is shorter term. The length of service, generally, has been reduced by about one-third within this century to about seven years—longer in private than in public institutions. The role is less academic—more academic decisions are made by the faculties, and, within the administration, the role of provost has grown greatly in importance—presidents were once their own provosts. The creation of the provostship (or academic vice presidency) and the rise of provosts as the new persons of power on campus is one of the least recognized but most significant changes of all. Presidents seldom teach anymore—once upon a time they were expected to teach the most central course of all in moral philosophy. Their role is more bureaucratic, and administrative staffs have grown much faster than academic, often twice or three times as fast. The role is also more one of external representation.

The role of the spouse has changed even more. Once it was that of the "minister's wife." Now it still sometimes is, but it is also by now so varied that it can only be described by a case-by-case approach.[21] Agonies of decision making about roles and about in-course adjustments result, and there is much confusion.

The general context for the exercise of authority has also changed from respect to challenge. "Followers" are more diverse and less passive. And the president is less engaged in exercising authority and more in assembling consent issue by issue—in "agreement building," to use a phrase from John Gardner.

Approaching the Presidency in the 1990s

The basic answer to the question of how to approach the presidency in the 1990s is: "With caution." But that has long been true. Colleges and universities (and, in particular, medical schools within them) are the most complex institutions in our society, much more so than corporations or trade unions or government agencies or foundations. The other organizations closest in complexity are hospitals and schools. Colleges and universities are a series of more-or-less separate "estates"[22] inhabiting the same spaces and experiencing shared fates, but with both harmonious and conflicting methods of governance, mentalities, purposes. The president is related to each estate but in control of none, except perhaps the bureaucracy. The 1990s will require some variations on the old theme of taking a cautious approach to these and other complexities. What may some of these variations be?

More than ever it is important to look at the presidency as an episode in life and not as life itself. This means being concerned with exit as well as with entrance; with the presidency as one stage in a career; with negotiating the terms of exit along with those of entrance. One should also give thought to the likely lifeline of the presidency when it goes through its customary phases[23] of initial acceptance with high hopes (possibly the first two years), of adequate but less-enthusiastic support (possibly the next three years), and of accumulating grievances as the law of accumulating grievances takes over (possibly a final two years);[24] but always with the chance of the "eternal life" that comes to a favored few in favored situations—eternal life now defined as lasting more than ten years.

One should also look at oneself more carefully than in earlier times: at one's willingness to work in complex circumstances without clear and agreed-upon goals and tests of performance, at one's endurance to participate in endless consultations and to postpone satisfactions, at one's ability to accept conflict as natural and eternal but with the faith that it is often subject to constructive resolutions. Also, at one's ability to understand and work with irrational as well as with rational behaviors, as the passions around the new issues become as important as the older interests of individuals and groups.[25] And, also, at one's realistic willingness to sacrifice institutional autonomy to intervention by the courts, state agencies, and even the police; to be more a part of society and to be less apart from society than we once thought we were and preferred being—this may be by now just pure nostalgia. Also at one's ability to accept at least postponement of the great "dream" of integration.

One should also look more carefully at the spousal relationship within the context of the job. What will it be? Will it survive the inherent tensions? Are there adequate institutional resources to support the public affairs role without undue hardship for the president and the spouse, or the president alone if there is no participating spouse?

One should also look more carefully at the team in place or to be assembled, and particularly at the provost, the dean of students, the legal counsel, and the public relations officer—who along with the president are most often on the front lines. Not that the vice president of business (once number two on campus and occasionally number one) or the budget officer are no longer important, but they are comparatively less so. In particular, to the extent that faculty participation in shared governance declines, the importance of the role of the provost increases.[26]

One should also look at the flow of information in order to be alert to developing changes: at the magazines and books to read; at the conferences to attend; at the people to consult; at the groups to meet. No longer is it enough to talk occasionally with the president of the student body or the chair of the faculty senate—not in a world of fractionated groups. It is more important that the president "walk" the campus or have someone "walk" it for her or him.

One should look carefully at board/president relationships as a cornerstone for stability in the midst of stress, and at faculty/president relations.

I once wrote, in *The Uses of the University,* that a president was a mediator, an initiator, a gladiator.[27] The 1990s look to me a time more for the first of these three roles, rephrased as that of an agreement builder, as the campus becomes increasingly multipolar and as conflict increases between and among the several poles.

Let me conclude, having said all of the above, with three comments. (1) Leadership, in the special situations within higher education, is becoming both more important and more difficult. (2) Most presidents that I interviewed and that were interviewed by my colleagues in the studies for the Association of Governing Boards—over one thousand—looked at the presidency as the greatest single challenge of their lives, their best chance to grow in knowledge and skills, and their preeminent chance to make significant contributions. (3) Fortunately, most persons interested in presidencies are not risk-aversive. On the contrary, they are risk takers. It is the risk takers who have given American higher education such comparatively dynamic leadership. And it is remarkable how many high-quality risk takers continue to be available to take leadership.

There are twenty-four hundred presidents today of nonspecialized colleges and universities—a favored, but not always entirely happy, few, who have a special opportunity to contribute to the maintenance and even the enhancement of such important institutions in our society—to make a difference to their institutions and in their own lives.

In approaching the 1990s, it is well to remember the observation of Heraclitus twenty-five hundred years ago: "It is not possible to step twice into the same river." The 1990s will be a different river, as each of the other decades before it has also been. Each river presents its own challenges.

Notes

1. "But when the trustees' admiration for the occupants of the vice-presidential level grows without a corresponding increase in good feeling for the president, a trustee may muse about the president's usefulness, as has this Cummings trustee: 'Maybe Cummings College doesn't need a president. A college can run very effectively with the top administrators and the [senate of] the faculty' " (Miriam Mason Wood, *Trusteeship in the Private College* [Baltimore: Johns Hopkins Press, 1985], 16).

2. Clark Kerr, "Shaping the Future of Board-Presidential Leadership," in *Shaping the Future of Higher Education: Presidential Leadership,* Proceedings of the

American Association of State Colleges and Universities Twenty-ninth Annual Meeting, San Francisco, 19–21 November 1989 (Washington, D.C.: American Association of State Colleges and Universities, 1990), 48–53. Reprinted by permission.

3. Clark Kerr, "Conversation on the Changing Role of the President," (Speech presented at the annual meeting of the American Council on Education, San Francisco, 17 January 1991; introduced by John W. Gardner).

4. Clark Kerr, "Higher Education Leadership in the Year 2000" (Speech presented at the Nineteenth Annual Conference of the National Center for the Study of Collective Bargaining in Higher Education and the Professions, San Francisco, 14 March 1991).

5. Jacques Barzun, *Being Here* (Chicago: University of Chicago Press, 1991), 193.

6. This observation is usually credited to Bill J. Priest, long-time president of American River College in California and of the Dallas County Community College District.

7. National Commission on Strengthening Presidential Leadership (Clark Kerr, Chair), *Presidents Make a Difference: Strengthening Leadership in Colleges and Universities* (Washington, D.C.: Association of Governing Boards of Universities & Colleges, 1984); Clark Kerr and Marian L. Gade, *The Many Lives of Academic Presidents: Time, Place, and Character* (Washington, D.C.: Association of Governing Boards of Universities & Colleges, 1986); Clark Kerr and Marian L. Gade, *The Guardians: Boards of Trustees of American Colleges and Universities—What They Do and How Well They Do It* (Washington, D.C.: Association of Governing Boards of Universities & Colleges, 1989).

8. James G. March, "How We Talk and How We Act: Administrative Theory and Administrative Life," Seventh David D. Henry Lecture, University of Illinois, September 1980, in *Values, Leadership, and Quality: The Administration of Higher Education* (Urbana: University of Illinois Press, 1990), 47.

9. See the discussion in Herbert J. Muller, *Uses of the Past* (New York: Shocken, 1985), 374.

10. Michael D. Cohen and James G. March, *Leadership and Ambiguity: The American College President* (New York: McGraw-Hill, 1974), 82.

11. A survey by the Carnegie Foundation for the Advancement of Teaching, reported in *The Chronicle of Higher Education* 31, no. 8 (23 October 1985).

12. Cohen and March, *Leadership and Ambiguity*, 24.

13. See the National Commission on Strengthening Presidential Leadership, *Presidents Make a Difference*.

14. There are, of course, other models to choose among as current tendencies evolve, including these: the moderator of the campus community trying mostly to keep the peace; the ambassador to the external world seeking to get funds and protect autonomy; the minister of morality concerned with ethical issues.

15. Cohen and March, *Leadership and Ambiguity*, 149.

16. Thorstein Veblen, *Higher Learning in America: A Memorandum on the Conduct of Universities by Businessmen* (Stanford, Calif.: Academic Reprints, 1954); originally published in 1918.

17. Cohen and March, *Leadership and Ambiguity*, chap. 5.

18. Robert K. Greenleaf, *Servant Leadership: A Journey into the Nature of Legitimate Power and Greatness* (New York: Paulist Press, 1977).

19. John W. Gardner, *On Leadership* (New York: Free Press, 1990).

20. No one today would claim that the University of California was controlled by the "railroad trust" or the University of Oregon by the "lumber trust," as Upton Sinclair did. (See Upton Sinclair, *The Goose-Step: A Study of American Education* [New York: AMS Press, 1970]; originally published 1923.)

21. See, for example, Roberta H. Ostar, *Public Roles, Private Lives: The Representational Role of College and University Presidents* (Washington, D.C.: Association of Governing Boards of Universities & Colleges, 1990); Joan E. Clodius and Diane Skomars Magrath, eds., *The President's Spouse: Volunteer or Volunteered* (Washington, D.C.: National Association of State Universities & Land-Grant Colleges, 1984); and Marguerite Walker Corbally, *The Partners: Sharing the Life of a College President* (Danville, Ill.: Interstate, 1977).

22. See the discussion in Clark Kerr, *The Great Transformation in Higher Education, 1960–1980* (Albany: State University of New York Press, 1991), Introduction to part 3.

23. For a "stage theory" of the presidency, see Robert Birnbaum, "Will You Love Me in December as You Do in May?: Why Experienced College Presidents Lose Faculty Support," *Journal of Higher Education* 63, no. 1 (January-February 1992): 1–25.

24. The most customary faculty grievances are (1) that there are too few resources obtained and (2) that there is too much interference in the affairs of the faculty estate, which so prizes its autonomy.

25. See the discussion in Albert O. Hirschman, *The Passions and the Interests* (Princeton: Princeton University Press, 1977).

26. I favor the president's also serving as provost, as presidents historically have at Harvard, and as they once did at Berkeley, with appropriate staff assistance. Among other things, this puts the president in close direct contact with shared governance.

Ideally, also, the president (or provost) should serve on every committee involving promotion for appointment to tenure. An alternative is meeting with the chair of any faculty-wide committee reviewing such promotion or appointment to seek assurance that a high-quality decision is being made. Let me note, as an important aside, that the provost has a particularly good opportunity—but other top officers do also—to develop an independent constituency and to become the "business agent" for this constituency versus the president and thus at least semi-independent from presidential influence. Personal compatibility and personal relations are of great importance in such situations and should be carefully considered in advance.

27. Clark Kerr, *The Uses of the University* (Cambridge: Harvard University Press, 1963, 1972, 1982). I now regret the use of the word *mediator*. It means to many the simple role of carrying messages back and forth. But the role in question is, in my experience, much more than that (see the discussion in Clark Kerr, "Industrial Conflict and Its Mediation," *American Journal of Sociology* 60, no. 3 [November 1954]: 230–45. And I have a very high opinion of successful mediators—the greatest of all in American history were those who developed the American Constitution, which is, itself, a great program for mediation in a highly pluralistic society.

PART II

Higher Education and the Economy:
An Increasingly Dominant Connection

Introduction: From God to Mammon

The main purposes of higher education have varied greatly from time to time and place to place around the world. Sometimes they have been service to the church, or to the ancient professions, or to an ideology, or to an aristocratic and/or affluent class, or to the efficiency and power of the nation-state. In modern times and in more and more places, the main purpose has come to be: to serve the economy. So it is currently in the United States.

A simplistic view, but an illuminating one, is that American higher education has been on a long journey of 350 years from serving God to serving Mammon. Harvard was founded "to advance learning and perpetuate it to Posterity; dreading to leave an illiterate Ministry to the Churches, when our present Ministers shall lie in the Dust."[1] Now it is said that "education [is] viewed by all three groups—business, academia, and government—as the key to the nation's competitiveness."[2] (See chapter 6.) How well it served God, particularly in the period from 1636 to the War between the States when this was considered the main purpose, is not subject to human proof. How well it now serves the economy is, however, open to some evidence. This segment of the book is devoted to analyzing this great shift from God to Mammon that is such an overwhelming aspect of higher education today—and the success of which, as appraised by society, is so important to the future welfare of higher education.

The essays that follow set forth how this shift in emphasis has come about and advance some cautions, particularly that this trend has by now, in my judgment, become excessive in relation to the other purposes of higher education.

Chapter 4 generally says that higher education has served well the American labor market, but at some costs to itself. Chapter 5 treats with university-corporate relations, which are mostly found to be within reasonable bounds, but there are inherent dangers. Chapters 6 and 7 look at the claimed failures of education in the United States to give adequate support to the economy and conclude that the asserted failures are not supported in fact—that there has been a gross miscarriage of common judgment.

Notes

1. "New England's First Fruits, 1643," in *American Higher Education: A Documentary History*, vol. 1, ed. Richard Hofstadter and Wilson Smith (Chicago: University of Chicago Press, 1961), 6.

2. The National Governors' Association and the Conference Board for the National Science Foundation, *The Role of Science and Technology in Economic Competitiveness* (Washington, D.C.: National Governors' Association, 1987).

CHAPTER 4

How Well Has Higher Education in the United States Met the Test of Service to the Labor Market?

This essay is on how well (or how badly) higher education has performed in serving the labor market and, through it, the economy. I think it has done very well, and would even go so far as to say as well as or better than anywhere else in the world. I would say about the American system of higher education in its totality what Henry Rosovsky has said about American research universities in particular:

> *In these days when foreign economic rivals seem to be surpassing us in one field after another, it may be reassuring to know that there is one vital industry where America unquestionably dominates the world: higher education. Between two-thirds and three-quarters of the world's best universities are located in the United States. This fact has been ignored by the many recent critics of higher education in America.*
>
> *What other sector of our economy can make a similar statement? There are baseball, football, and basketball teams—but that pretty much exhausts the list. No one has suggested that today America is home to two-thirds of the best steel mills, automobile factories, chip manufacturers, banks, or government agencies. Our position at the upper end of the quality scale in higher education is unusual, may be a special national asset, and needs to be explained.*
>
> *In higher education, 'made in America' still is the finest label. My only advice is to add 'handle with care,' lest we too descend to the level of most other American industrial performance.[1]*

I discuss five aspects of service to the labor market and give generally fair to good marks to each of them. My major reservations relate to the talent hunt, the transfer programs in community colleges, and three professional schools.

There are those who think that service to the labor market is something new to higher education. Jacques Barzun has written that "everybody knows what has happened to the university as an institution since World War II. It has moved from wherever it was to the center of the marketplace."[2] What everyone should also know is that is where it was for the Sophists in Athens and for the University of Bologna as the mother university of modern Western civilization and at most other times and places. The real questions are: How well does it perform this function, and what else should it be doing and in what proportions?

The Agora and the Acropolis

Many observers, beginning with Socrates in his attacks on the Sophists, have answered in the negative to the question of whether education should be useful:

> Plato: The purpose of education is "knowledge of beauty and goodness."[3]
>
> Matthew Arnold: The purpose of the university is to produce "sweetness and light" and not "engineers."[4]
>
> Robert Maynard Hutchins: The purpose of the university "is to provide a haven where the search for truth may go on unhampered by utility or pressure for 'results.' "[5]
>
> Abraham Flexner: The purpose of the university is not "the training of practical men." It is not a "dumping ground."[6]

My answer to the question is a qualified one: Contributions to the economy make up one purpose among several but should never become the only one.

Higher education, as a matter of fact, has always served the labor market in one way or another and to one degree or another. In fact, universities began in Europe in early modern times precisely for that purpose.

The University of Bologna (c. A.D. 1200) addressed the labor market needs of the expanding commercial revolution by supplying lawyers and judges, and administrators and accountants; and law and mathematics (along with Aristotelian philosophy) were the important subjects in the curriculum. It can even be said that the commercial revolution, first led by the Italian city-states, would have been far less successful without the early universities, and thus Italy had two competitive advantages in this revolution—its location in the center of the Mediterranean and its early development of universities. Bologna set the model for future universities by serving the ancient professions of law, teaching, and medicine (but not theology), adding, over time, engineering and service to scholarship, particularly in medicine and mathematics. The Bologna model, via Salamanca, to this day has been followed in the Hispanic nations, with their greatest emphasis being on the professional schools.

Paris (c. A.D. 1200) began with theology and philosophy and thus more with scholarship, but, as at Oxford and Cambridge, which followed its example, it also provided for the training of priests. Bologna and Paris were the original European models. The earlier Muslim model was also heavy on theology and the training of priests (as in Paris), but, in addition, on the preservation of Greek learning and on astronomy, mathematics, and geography.

The Napoleonic system in France (c. A.D. 1800), later emulated elsewhere, at first concentrated on supplying teachers to the educational system and civil servants to the state agencies, and French universities concentrate heavily on these assigned duties to this day. The Confucian educational system in China over many centuries also heavily emphasized training for the civil service and for teaching, as did the British system in India. The Humboldt model in Germany (c. A.D. 1800), later followed elsewhere, concentrated on scholarly research but also on the training of engineers, particularly in the technical universities. The British system began with the training of priests (later the Anglican clergy) but switched, over time, also to the training and perpetuation of an aristocracy—the reproduction of a ruling class, and a comparatively well-educated one. This is where the idea of a liberal education, as so beautifully expounded by Cardinal Newman, really began in modern times; the British system has had a comparative animus toward professional pursuits, continuing into the current era but now subject to strong governmental pressures for reversal. The historic British system has not been the world model, though it is much admired in nostalgic recollections of Oxford and Cambridge, but is rather the exception in turning its back on crass professionalism and service to money-making pursuits. It was once the "purest" of them all.

The socialist systems of higher education, beginning with the USSR after the end of World War I, heavily emphasized service to the labor market as part of an economic plan, and to ideological indoctrination as part of the political system, as Paris and Oxford and Cambridge and other universities in earlier times had also expounded what they considered the true faith. China, in more recent times, has swung violently from emphasis on ideology (the Cultural Revolution) to emphasis on the labor market (modernization). Japan has stayed steadily with a labor-market orientation ever since the Meiji Restoration after the middle of the nineteenth century.

This brief historical sketch is intended to make two points: (1) Service to the labor market has been from the start an important part of higher education in most of the world and has continued to be so at nearly all times and in nearly all places—this emphasis is not a recent descent from the Olympian heights of scholarship but quite the contrary; and (2) it has, however, nearly always been only one function that took its place, now greater and now lesser, along with other functions—sometimes complementing these other functions and sometimes competing with them.

The cherished view of some academics that higher education started out on the acropolis of scholarship and was desecrated by descent into the agora of materialistic pursuits led by ungodly commercial interests, scheming public officials, and venal academic leaders is just not true for the university systems that have developed at least since A.D. 1200. If anything, higher education started in the agora, the marketplace, at the bottom of the hill, sometimes gradually, as in Italy, and sometimes in a big leap, as in Germany. Mostly, it has lived in tension, at one and the same time at the bottom of the hill, at the top of the hill, and on the many pathways in between. One of the great tensions in higher education today in many nations is the conflict between what some academics think should happen on the top of the hill and what actually goes on in response to the marketplace down below. There is no Golden Age today of pure scholarship alone, and there never was one. The closest approximations were the Lyceum and Atheneum in ancient Greece and the Newman model when, to some extent, it prevailed in England; but these were the great exceptions. To the extent that there has been a fall from grace, it has been from grace in only a few places and at only a few times. Even in ancient Greece, the Sophists attracted more students than Socrates, Plato, and Aristotle.

The American system began with the twin purposes of preserving civilized ways of thought in the wilderness and of training ministers.

Until about the time of the War between the States, American colleges mostly continued to advance civilization (liberal education) and to prepare students as an educated element in society preparatory to entering the historic professions of teaching and the ministry, and law and medicine—often via apprenticeships. Three great surges of activity later put more stress on the labor market side: the land-grant movement with its emphasis on preparing engineers and other "useful" professionals, thus advancing production in industry and agriculture; the transformation of teachers' colleges into comprehensive colleges and universities, training mostly for occupations more tied to distribution and to consumption services; and the rise of the community colleges, concentrated mostly on vocational skills. Along with an emphasis on research, particularly after the War between the States and taken from the Humboldt model, these developments created the modern American system of higher education. The movement, net, has been toward more multifaceted economic contributions to the society at large with comparatively less interest than before the War between the States in the ancient professions for the sake of service to the middle classes and in civilized discourse within the upper middle classes (liberal learning).

What is new is not that higher education in the United States has fallen from grace as the Captains of Industry have led the Captains of Erudition by the nose, and they, in turn, have led their serfs down the garden paths into ways of iniquity, as Veblen saw it.[7] What is new, rather, is that much more of the work force is introduced into productive labor via higher education (now 45 percent in the United States, versus 1 to 2 percent in 1870); and that this new work force serves the interests of all of the population, rather than those of the more educated classes alone, in staying well (medicine), staying out of trouble (law), getting into heaven (theology), and getting a liberal education and becoming a "gentleman" (teaching). If all this is a loss to higher education—which requires proof—it clearly has advantaged the population as a whole. Earlier elitist systems of higher education in the United Kingdom and in America more nearly served a small part of the population. Mass systems more nearly serve all of the people.

How Has Higher Education Performed?

1. Higher education in the United States currently oversupplies the labor market. The Carnegie Commission made a "very rough guess" that about one in eight college-educated persons were, and prospectively might be, located in jobs that did not require their levels of formal education and that these jobs had not been, and perhaps could not be, upgraded to make use of it.[8] The *Workforce 2000* report of the Hudson Institute more recently estimated that 42 percent of jobs "required" one or more years of college education[9] as against 45 percent of persons in the labor force with this level of education or above. This implies a "surplus" of about one in fifteen. A difficulty is, however, that employed persons' having a certain level of education does not necessarily mean that this level is "required." It also does not mean that persons with a higher educational level cannot make good use of it on the job, even though minimum requirements for performance might be met with a lower educational level.[10]

This extra one-eighth or one-fifteenth is not necessarily a loss to society. It puts downward pressure on wage differentials, as compared with what might otherwise happen, which helps to increase equality of income and to equalize net satisfaction from jobs. People in this extra one-eighth or one-fifteenth also, on the average, benefit by better care of their health, by higher levels of savings and better quality of investments, and in other ways, just as do others who attend college.[11] And additional people are given a chance to advance themselves, whether it pays off or not.

This apparent surplus implies that the capacity and the inclination both exist within higher education to meet the rising skill needs of the American economy between now and the year 2000, recently estimated in the Hudson Institute study to rise from 42 percent of the labor force to 52 percent of new entrants by 2000 (44 percent of the total labor force as of that date) for persons with one or more years of education beyond high school; and 30 percent of new entrants between now and 2000 are estimated to require four years or more of college.[12]

My own judgment is that these estimates of *Workforce 2000* are about right. I would note that 30 percent of the employed population is now in managerial, scientific, and technical occupations, which can generally make use of a college education; and that another roughly 20 percent can make use of education beyond high school for labor-market purposes, including in community colleges, proprietary schools, and, to some extent, the military. Actually, 47 percent of the existing labor force has attended college for one year or more, and 27 percent for four years or more.[13]

Some college attendance serves primarily a holding function of waiting until something better comes along,[14] including as an alternative to unemployment or to a marginally acceptable job. Other reasons for the tendency to create an oversupply to the labor market include these: the public subsidy of higher education so that the private costs of attendance are often far less than the total costs of education; the pressure of parents themselves with higher education to have their children attend colleges and universities—and the pressure keeps building over the generations; and, some places, the pressure by members of peer groups on those otherwise marginally motivated to attend.

Any modest oversupply does not mean that we have a problem of "the overeducated American." This thesis was advanced on the grounds that the comparative rate of return on a college education was going down (as of 1974) from the high point of 1969.[15] But the rate of return has since risen again and is substantial,[16] and there are many other benefits to a college education, as we have already noted and will note further below. Freeman's view reflected, in part, the economic conditions of the early 1970s with recessions and depressions, and with the baby-boom generation entering the labor market. Jacob Mincer more recently has labeled the claim that we have an overeducated population as a "myth."[17]

Daniel Bell, in an article outlining possibilities for the year 2013, estimated that "more than half the labor force is in white-collar, middle-class, and education-requiring categories."[18] More specifically he saw a "four tiered system" taking shape:

a. An upper middle class of professional and managerial workers, comprising about 25 percent of the population;
b. a middle class of technical, administrative support, and skilled workers, representing 35 percent of the population;
c. a service class, being about 25 percent of the population; and
d. an underclass of about 15 percent, comprising individuals with no steady employment, doing odd jobs, menial labor, and the like.[19]

This suggests that higher education will need to serve about 60 percent of the labor force in that still dimly foreseeable future, rather than 45 percent; that the high school graduation rate will need to be 85 percent, a level of educational attainment now reached by the younger cohorts in the labor force; and that in the process there will be created a more clearly stratified society. But even if these proportions come true, it is likely that the American system of higher education will still be creating a surplus of attendees above labor-market requirements, as it does today and for the reasons already given. Basically, supply follows demand.

Overall, the American system of higher education is very responsive to overall labor-market needs, and this is a great asset to the economy.[20]

2. Higher education helps to sort out and to distribute workers into the labor market in a relatively effective way, but there are distortions. There is no evidence that major deficits for college-trained persons, occupational category by occupational category, have existed over substantial lengths of time, with one or two possible major exceptions. At one time, the 1960s, when the medical profession still greatly influenced the size of medical school classes, it was widely thought that there was a deficit of doctors, and this was also at a time when the distribution of medical care was undergoing a massive extension under federal policies. And while the incomes of medical doctors were comparatively quite high, this was substantially due to the long hours they worked,[21] and not alone to control of entrance to the trade. When the federal government, the states, and the universities took control of places available on a "planning" basis, the result, if anything, has been a surplus of doctors.

Putting higher education into the labor-market process for over 40 percent of the population generally does, however, introduce a certain sluggishness in response of supply to demand. The adjustment process becomes more complex, and lags are introduced between demand and supply. In earlier times, most persons wanting a job went directly to the place of employment after high school or even after grammar school. Now over 40 percent of job seekers are subject to a lag of one or two or four or five or more years between deciding what type of employment they think they want, considering the demand at the time they start out in college (many, of course, change expectations along the way), and the time they emerge as supply. Thus "cobweb cycle" situations result, as for engineers.[22] Low entering salaries for engineers reduce entrants into engineering schools. Later, when the small cohort reaches the market, it does not meet demand, and entering salaries rise, which encourages many more students to enter, which, in turn, still later again reduces entering salaries, and the cycle begins all over again. These lags may help partially to explain Eckaus's finding that returns to education are not equalized over occupations as would be expected if the labor market worked to perfection.[23]

The supply of and demand for Ph.D.'s is a special case of a long-run tendency to oversupply. This reflects the intense interest of so many graduate students in their studies and their overexpectations about their own talents

TABLE 3

College Entrance Rates: High School Class of 1980

Socioeconomic status		Ability	
	Low	Medium[a]	High
Low	31	49	70
Medium[a]	N.A.	54	81
High	44	68	87

Source: Data developed by Norton Grubb from the National Longitudinal Studies of the high school class of 1980.

[a]Middle two quartiles

and about projected job opportunities in the distant future. It also reflects exploitation within universities. Departments get cheap and noncompetitive labor for teaching lower-division students. Faculty members also like the lower teaching loads that go with graduate assistants and the help they get with their research, and institutions seeking to rise in status like to call themselves "universities." Consequently, faculty members and their departments have a tendency to induce students to enter and stay in graduate study beyond the level of related job opportunities.[24] A special period of some temporary deficits may arise, however, from 1995 to 2005 for special demographic reasons.[25]

Overall, however, market forces work at an acceptable level. Margaret S. Gordon has noted the "considerable degree of student responsiveness to changes in relative job opportunities,"[26] and Richard B. Freeman the "responsive supply behavior on the part of young students" who "are highly sensitive in their educational and career decisions to the state of the labor market."[27] And higher education institutions, in turn, are very responsive to their student markets.[28]

In any event, there is no acceptable alternative in the United States to reliance on market forces, even delayed as responses often are in their operation by the introduction of higher education, and distorted as they sometimes are.

3. The talent hunt misses some talent. Dael Wolfle once found that among young people in the top one-fifth of academic talent, as identified by standardized tests, the loss in college attendance was about 10 percent if the loss is calculated as the increase that would occur if attendance rates of young people with high ability but from median- and lower-socioeconomic-status families were to attend at the same rate as from high-income families. More current data (1980) again show a loss of about 10 percent (table 3). This loss of talent, historically, has been heavily concentrated among women and mi-

TABLE 4

**Years of School Completed by Employed Persons
25 Years Old and Over—March 1989**

	Percent high school graduates	Percent 1 year college or more	Percent 4 years college or more
All occupations, races, both sexes	86.1	46.8	26.8
Males	84.4	48.0	28.7
Females	88.1	45.3	24.5
White males	85.2	48.7	29.4
White females	88.7	45.4	24.6
Black males	75.5	35.2	14.8
Black females	81.4	38.4	17.4
Spanish origin males	55.2	27.7	12.4
Spanish origin females	65.1	30.4	13.4

Source: U.S. Bureau of the Census, "Educational Attainment in the U.S.: March 1989 and 1988," *Current Population Reports, Population Characteristics,* ser. P-20, no. 451, Washington, D.C., August 1991, table 6.

norities. Today, however, a great advantage the United States has, as against other nations except the Nordic countries, is its greater educational opportunities for and integration of women into the labor market. White women, nevertheless, still do not match white men in graduate school attendance, and underserved minorities do not match them at any level.

Justice requires that talent from any source be given equal opportunity, and the economy can be a substantial gainer. As an indication of the potential for augmented contributions by higher education, additions to the labor force between now and 2000 are estimated to be 29 percent nonwhite and 64 percent female.[30] (For the 1989 distribution of educational attainment by sex and race, see table 4.) Opportunities for overcoming deficits in the talent hunt have been set back recently, however, by the changes in federal student aid policy from grants to loans. The talent-hunt process—these very major exceptions aside[31]—seems to have worked reasonably well, with the education system mostly identifying and sending forward the abler students.

The demographic condition of higher education in the 1990s, with a reduced growth rate of students from the traditional college-going cohort, offers particular opportunities to mitigate these exceptions by serving better those thus far underserved.[32] I consider this the greatest potential service over the next decade that higher education could render the economy, could make to the quality of individual lives, could provide to bolster the democratic strength of our political system, and could contribute to the American dream of equality of opportunity. Underserved minority groups now constitute

15 percent of our total population and 20 percent of our youth. Above all, education in the 1990s should be dedicated to this cause of substantial improvement.

Higher education seems to be responding quite well to the needs of older persons for more training for occupational purposes to change jobs or to advance in an established career pattern. Two of the fastest-growing segments of higher education have been the enrollment of older persons and the addition of programs at the M.A. level. As the labor force ages, this can be a great contribution to the economy.

4. The quality of the content of higher education for labor-market purposes is generally acceptable—with exceptions. Quality is, however, very difficult to measure. Reported employer judgments are about the only evidence in addition to test scores out of college, which do not generally show the same decline as out of high school.

Specialized skills generally seem to be provided at a satisfactory level and in some areas, such as science and engineering, at a superior level. The three areas that I would most fault, based upon my own experience and the reported experiences of many others, are business administration, engineering, and education; each will be discussed below.

5. Other labor-market contributions of higher education are generally positive. Other labor-market contributions of higher education include:

> Better health of college graduates compared to nonattenders.
> More mobility in the labor market.
> More women in the labor market, particularly after age forty, when the rate for college graduates is 50 percent higher than for non-college-graduates.
> More acceptance of and tolerance toward minority groups in the labor force, without which integration of the labor force would have been more difficult.
> More participation in political processes, a tendency toward more moderate positions on issues, and more willingness to accept change.
> A higher level of personal savings among college graduates, a better record with investments, and more efficient consumption practices.[33]
> More satisfaction on the job.[34]

A further widespread consequence for the economy is that the quality of working life becomes a much large consideration in the conduct of employment relationships as the labor force becomes more highly educated.

These side effects should be taken into account when calculating the economic and noneconomic effects of higher education.

How Might Higher Education Perform Better?

How might higher education perform better? First, I believe it should concentrate first and foremost on improvements in the performance of our community colleges, particularly in their remedial skills programs, in their programs to prepare students to transfer to four-year institutions, and in their advice and aid to young persons generally on the advancement of their lives and careers.[35]

Transfer programs have not developed as once anticipated in and encouraged by the 1960 Master Plan in California, and strongly recommended by the Carnegie Commission on Higher Education.[36] It has been suggested that this is because of the "diverted dream"—"a policy to channel students away from" four-year institutions in order to accord with "a class structure with limited room at the top,"[37] thus also advancing "the transmission of inequality from generation to generation."[38] All this influenced by the corporate structure of the United States.

I have seen no such concerted deliberate effort to subvert equality of opportunity—quite the contrary. I see other forces at work: the desire of the community colleges to respond to their developing markets for vocational and recreational courses, the response of students to vastly increased student aid by going directly to four-year institutions rather than using transfer programs, the response of some minority students in particular to use military service as their transfer route into a four-year college, and the vast increase in numbers of older students not interested in transfer programs. Also, the 1970s and 1980s were a period of increasing vocationalism in American higher education spreading throughout nearly all types of institutions, including the community colleges. By the end of the 1980s, however, 20 percent of all undergraduate degree recipients in the University of California system, and 50 percent in the California State University system, had transferred from community colleges. Thus the community colleges in California were a major means of upward mobility within higher education.[39]

Community colleges are now located within commuting distance of the vast majority of all Americans. Five million persons a year register for courses within them on a voluntary basis. These colleges also provide many cultural programs for their local communities. This has resulted in the most impressive opening up of opportunities for higher education and cultural advancement in the whole history of American higher education. These colleges, while not matching the high expectations of the California Master Plan or the Carnegie Commission, have been more a means of democratization within the total society than a means of diversion within a solidified class structure. In states with strong community college systems, more young people get four-year degrees than in states with weak systems.[40] Yet more can and should be done.

Second, at the four-year and advanced levels, higher education should concentrate attention on these professional fields:

Business administration. Since much of the decline in the rate of growth in productivity is traceable to management, schools of business administration must share some of the blame. My own view is that, among other deficiencies, they greatly neglect the human relations side of management at an historical stage of production when it becomes ever more important to associate the minds of employees, as well as their bodies, with their work. In content, business schools also greatly overemphasize marketing, advertising, and financing as against production management. One large school of business administration that I know well has only one out of fifty undergraduate courses in production management and only one out of one hundred graduate courses in the same area, and only one and two courses, respectively, in the management of human resources.

Another difficulty with schools of business administration is that they seek too avidly to respond to what their students demand and to what prospective employers seem to want, and too little to the real needs of the modern economy. They also have not been as critical of shortcomings in American management as schools of law have been about our system of justice or schools of medicine about health care. They respond too much, and they lead too little. Additionally, they have been a less integrative intellectual force within the social sciences than they might well have been.

Engineering. Engineering also neglects production management on the plant floor, where we need many more individuals well trained in this specialty. The college of engineering in one of the nation's outstanding research universities has seen an historic decline in nuts-and-bolts engineering, and only 7 courses out of 250 now relate to shop floor production. This may be inevitable, and even desirable, in a research university, but not in all institutions offering instruction in engineering, although MIT and Berkeley are both moving toward a greater emphasis on production engineering. The comprehensive colleges and universities can make a particular contribution in this area of expertise.

Also, as in the area of business management, the focus is still too much on the individual job and on rewards to the individual worker (Taylorism), and too little on performance by the team and rewards to the team. The United States has done best in past and current times in knowing, and the Japanese in knowing how; the Japanese are now catching up in the former, and the Americans must equally catch up in the latter—colleges of engineering are in the front lines, as are also schools of business.

Education. Schools of education, in my judgment, have been correctly criticized for the ineffectiveness of their teaching activities as well as for the low quality of most of their research. But they are very hard to change. James B. Conant, who led studies of the nation's high schools under Carnegie auspices for ten years, once advised me, when I was undertaking studies of higher education under the same auspices, to "never waste your time giving advice to schools of education." Nevertheless, my advice is that too many required courses of little value drive out some of the potentially best students in advance. I would do away with all undergraduate courses and have only two graduate-level courses required of all students—one in learning and one in teaching. In addition, graduate students in their first year would have jobs as teacher's assistants. In their second year, they would be practice teachers with concurrent discussion seminars in the same areas of problems of learning and problems of teaching. Half of the states now do have alternative programs to secure a teaching credential.

In particular, I would argue that schools of education are, in fact, "schools of schooling," but that education takes place in several major locations: the family, the school, the workplace, the media; and that schools of education should be studying the quality of contributions that take place in each of these locations and the relationships among them.

I would also argue that schools of education should be modeled more after schools of agriculture and less after schools of letters and science,[41] with field-oriented experiment stations and extension services.

Derek Bok, as president of Harvard, in recent annual reports, has given special attention to the professional schools of education and business, and also of law.[42]

What Impacts Does Service to the Labor Market Have on Higher Education?

Two major historical changes have taken place in the relationships of the labor market to higher education: (1) the extension of the use of higher education from supplying trained personnel for the ancient professions to supplying hundreds, and even thousands, of subprofessions and occupations and vocations; and (2) the related long-run greater perceived comparative importance of labor-market contributions, among the several functions of higher education. Higher education has been greatly affected.

The greater emphasis in higher education on labor-market functions is due not only to the changing requirements of the economy for more and more skills. It is also due to the changing expectations of students, at least in recent times in the United States but apparently elsewhere as well, that higher education, above all else, will prepare them successfully for entry into the labor market. Increasingly, the overwhelming expectation of American students for their higher education is to be "very well off financially"—75 percent in 1989, as against 45 percent in 1966.[43] As of 1989, 76 percent of respondents listed "to be able to get a better job" as highest among reasons for going to college.[44]

The consequences for higher education in the United States are substantial:

Enrollments have shifted heavily to professional schools, and the humanities and social sciences, in particular, have lost. Undergraduate enrollment in the professions rose from 38 to 58 percent between 1969 and 1975 alone, and in the humanities and social sciences taken together fell from 27 to 13 percent.[45]

Faculty distributions have also been shifted more heavily to professional fields, where there are often faster promotions and higher salary levels, thus creating internal tensions in the process.

The labor market, rather than academic policy, for a very long time, but particularly in the 1970s and 1980s, has been the major determinant of what students study, and part of this has resulted from the default of the faculties in their concerns for academic policy.

Higher education's contributions to advancement of the economy appear more useful to many corporate and political leaders, and to the public at large, and financial support consequently is more adequate than it otherwise would be.

Radical political action by faculty and students has greatly subsided—both students and professors in professional fields are generally more conservative politically. Other forces, of course, have also been at work.

Intrusion into what were once the internal affairs of higher education has increased. Affirmative action policies originally specifically intended for the labor market have also been introduced into higher education as a set of intrusions strongly related to the labor market. Also, governors insist more and more that higher education raise skills and help to create new jobs.

Administrators too often argue now the economic contributions of higher education to localities and regions and the nation as a whole, to the exclusion of other contributions. Leaders of higher education in the United States have too often asserted that their institutions are at the center of the rise and decline of the nation. Higher education in several countries, and perhaps particularly in the United States, has helped to

oversell itself in the process of gaining greater financial support. It may
end up having sold itself into a mild form of serfdom as well.

Higher education, nevertheless, more than ever before, does help create
the wealth that finances it.

I conclude that higher education has done more net for the economy than
the economy has done net for a balanced and autonomous system of higher
education. I also conclude that higher education needs to be clearer about
what it really can do to improve the productive functions of society, and to be
more thoughtful about what it is willing to do.

What can higher education do to protect itself? To begin with it can
present realistic rather than exaggerated expectations for additional contributions to the economy. And it can also seek to preserve its autonomy, including
its control over the total balance of its endeavors.

If any single external influence can now be said to dominate higher education in the United States, it is service to the economy through production
of higher skills and new advances in knowledge. This is also true of primary
and secondary education in the area of basic skills. But education at all levels, important as it is for many reasons, is not as central to the rise and fall
of our national economy as much public policy now seems to assume. It is
only one moderately important part in a tangled web of causes that still holds
its mysteries.

Notes

This chapter is a major revision of my articles "The Employment of University
Graduates in the United States," in *La Professionalisation de l'enseignement su-
perieur*, ed. Alain Bienayme, Ladislav Cerych, and Guy Neave; the proceedings of a
conference held at the University of Paris IX-Dauphine, June 1984, under the auspices
of the European Institute of Education (Paris: Institut Européen d'Education et de
Politique Sociale, Université de Paris IX-Dauphine, 1985) and "A General Perspective on Higher Education and Service to the Labor Market," *Policy Perspectives*, no.
1 (September 1988), Paper Abstracts pp. 1–2, reprinted by permission of the University of Pennsylvania.

1. Henry Rosovsky, "Highest Education," *The New Republic*, 13 and 20 July
1987, pp. 13–14. Quoted by permission.

2. Jacques Barzun, *Being Here* (Chicago: University of Chicago Press, 1991),
156.

3. Plato, *Republic*, book 6.

4. Matthew Arnold, *Culture and Anarchy: An Essay in Political and Social Criticism*, ed. with introduction and notes by Ian Gregor (Indianapolis: Bobbs-Merrill,
1971), 17; originally published in 1869.

5. Robert Maynard Hutchins, *The Higher Learning in America* (New Haven: Yale University Press, 1936), 43.

6. Abraham Flexner, *Universities: American, English, German* (London: Oxford University Press, 1968), 27; originally published in 1930.

7. Thorstein Veblen, *Higher Learning in America: A Memorandum on the Conduct of Universities by Businessmen* (Stanford, Calif.: Academic Reprints, 1954); first published in 1918.

8. Carnegie Commission on Higher Education, *College Graduates and Jobs* (New York: McGraw-Hill, 1973), 4.

9. William B. Johnston, *Workforce 2000* (Indianapolis: Hudson Institute, 1987), 98.

10. See the discussion in Lewis C. Solmon, "New Findings on the Links between College Education and Work," *Higher Education* 10, no. 6 (1981): 627. Also see Lewis C. Solmon, Ann J. Bisconti, and Nancy L. Ochsner, *College as a Training Ground for Jobs* (New York: Praeger, 1977).

11. See F. Thomas Juster, ed., *Education, Income, and Human Behavior* (New York: McGraw-Hill, 1975).

12. Johnston, *Workforce 2000*. Calculated from table 3–8 and data on pp. 98 and 99.

13. U.S. Bureau of the Census, "Educational Attainment in the United States: March 1989 and 1988," *Current Population Reports*, ser. P-20, no. 451 (1991), table 6.

14. Burton R. Clark, "The 'Cooling-Out' Function in Higher Education," *The American Journal of Sociology* 65, no. 6, (1960): 569–76.

15. See Richard B. Freeman, *The Overeducated American* (New York: Academic Press, 1976), 14.

16. Kevin Murphy and Finis Welch ("Wage Premiums of College Graduates," *Educational Researcher* 18, no. 4 [May 1989]:17–26) show a high rate of 1.61 in 1971, a low rate of 1.48 in 1979, and a new high rate of 1.67 in 1986. See also McKinley L. Blackburn, David E. Bloom, and Richard B. Freeman, "An Era of Falling Earnings and Rising Inequality?" *Brookings Review* 9, no. 1 (Winter 1990/91): 38–43.

17. Jacob Mincer, "Comment: Overeducation or Undereducation," in *Education and Economic Activity*, ed. Edwin Dean (Cambridge, Mass: Ballinger, 1984), 208.

18. Daniel Bell, "The World and the United States in 2013," *Daedalus* 116, no. 3 (Summer 1987): 27.

19. Ibid., 26.

20. This may be particularly true for the period ahead to the year 2000. Total employment is expected to rise by 15 percent, but employment in the more "educated" occupations is expected to rise as follows:

- Executive, administrative, and managerial occupations: 22 percent
- Professional specialty occupations: 24 percent
- Technicians and related support occupations: 32 percent

(See George Silvestri and John Lukasiewicz, "Projections of Occupational Employment, 1988–2000," *Monthly Labor Review* 112, no. 11 [November 1989]: 42–65.)

21. See Richard S. Eckaus, *Estimating the Returns to Education* (Berkeley: Carnegie Commission on Higher Education, 1973).

22. See the discussion in Freeman, *The Overeducated American,* chap. 5; also in *idem, The Market for College Trained Manpower* (Cambridge: Harvard University Press, 1971).

23. Eckaus, *Estimating the Returns to Education,* 52–53.

24. See the discussion in David W. Breneman, "The Ph.D. Production Process: A Study of Departmental Behavior" (Ph.D. diss., Department of Economics, University of California, Berkeley, 1970). Also see William G. Bowen and Neil Rudenstine, *In Pursuit of the Ph.D.* (Princeton: Princeton University Press, 1992), chap. 10.

25. See the discussion in William G. Bowen and Julie Ann Sosa, *Prospects for Faculty in the Arts and Sciences* (Princeton: Princeton University Press, 1989).

26. See Margaret S. Gordon, ed., *Higher Education and the Labor Market* (New York: McGraw-Hill, 1974), 7.

27. Freeman, *The Overeducated American,* 52–53.

28. See the discussion in David Riesman, *On Higher Education: The Academic Enterprise in an Era of Rising Consumerism* (San Francisco: Jossey-Bass, 1980).

29. Dael Wolfle, *The Uses of Talent* (Princeton: Princeton University Press, 1971), 105.

30. Johnston, *Work Force 2000,* 44, xxi.

31. Education is, however, the chief and even predominant source of progress for blacks. (See James P. Smith and Finis R. Welch, "Black Economic Progress after Myrdal," *Journal of Economic Literature* 27, no. 2 [June 1989]: 519–64.) See also the discussion of "the gradual growth of universalistic patterns of stratification and mobility" via education versus the influence of race, gender, and class in David B. Grusky, "Recent Trends in the Process of Stratification," (Department of Sociology, Stanford University, April 1989).

32. See the discussion in Arthur Levine and Associates, *Shaping Higher Education's Future* (San Francisco: Jossey-Bass, 1989).

33. For evidence, see, in particular, Juster, *Education, Income, and Human Behavior.* Also see Howard R. Bowen, *Investment in Learning: The Individual and Social Value of American Higher Education* (San Francisco: Jossey-Bass, 1977).

34. See, in particular, Solmon, Bisconti, and Ochsner, *College as a Training Ground for Jobs.* See also Solmon, "New Findings."

35. On the latter point, see the discussion in Carnegie Council on Policy Studies in Higher Education, *Giving Youth a Better Chance* (San Francisco: Jossey-Bass, 1979).

36. Carnegie Commission on Higher Education, *The Open-Door Colleges: Policies for Community Colleges* (New York: McGraw-Hill, 1970).

37. See the discussion in Steven Brint and Jerome Karabel, *The Diverted Dream* (New York: Oxford University Press, 1989), 213.

38. Ibid., 224.

39. More generally, one-quarter of all community-college students taking four courses or more later transferred to four-year colleges (Arthur M. Cohen and Florence Brawer, Press Release, Center for the Study of Community Colleges, Los Angeles, 7 May 1991).

40. Norton Grubb, "The Causes of Enrollment in Postsecondary Education: Evidence from the National Longitudinal Study of the Class of 1972," (National Center for Research in Vocational Education, University of California, Berkeley, October 1990).

41. With minidepartments of psychology, sociology, administration, history, philosophy, and so forth. Schools of education do need many specialty areas, such as remedial teaching, English as a second language, advising, and administration, in addition to an emphasis on learning and teaching in general.

42. See *The President's Report* (Harvard University) for 1977–78 on the business school, 1981–82 on the school of law, and 1985–86 on the school of education. Bok has also been critical of schools of social welfare and public administration (Derek Bok, *Universities and the Future of America* [Durham and London: Duke University Press, 1990]).

43. The 1989 figure is from Alexander W. Astin, *The American Freshman: National Norms for Fall 1989,* Los Angeles: Cooperative Institutional Research Program, UCLA (1990); the 1966 figure is from Alexander W. Astin, Robert J. Panos, and John A. Creager, *National Norms for Entering College Freshmen—Fall 1966* (Washington, D.C.: American Council on Education, Office of Research, 1967).

44. See Astin, *The American Freshman.*

45. Carnegie Foundation for the Advancement of Teaching, *Missions of the College Curriculum* (San Francisco: Jossey-Bass, 1977), 103.

CHAPTER 5

The Corporation and the University:
The American Experience

This essay is based on a presentation I made in Tokyo to an assembly of university presidents drawn heavily from Japan and the United States— the two industrial nations where corporate-university relations have been most highly developed.[1] But other nations, as a matter of policy, are currently seeking to increase cooperative arrangements between industries and universities, as, for example, in Great Britain and Italy— where hot arguments have ensued. Even in the United States, where controversies once raged[2] and then almost disappeared, new debates have recently arisen. Such relations are, at best, uneasy ones. Some goals are shared, but others are not; and there are eternal ethical issues.

Both the corporation and the campus have grown enormously in social importance in the United States, and in concert, over the past century and a quarter (1865–1990). They have also grown more apart from each other ideologically, while becoming more dependent on each other economically than ever before. How has this come to be?

After the War between the States, this country entered into a period of industrial expansion that has carried it to a position of world leadership. The corporations have been in the forefront of this expansion at home and even abroad. Abroad, the American corporations are said to be, in their totality, the third-greatest industrial power in the world.

Simultaneously, higher education in the United States experienced its greatest period of growth. The classical college gave way to the leadership of the public land-grant university and the private research university in response to political populism, economic growth in industry and agriculture, and the rise of science. The United States now has more universities of international stature, by far, than any other nation.

Today, the United States is a world leader both in per-capita income and in the higher education of its citizens. The corporation has substantial responsibility for the first accomplishment, and the university for the second.

Yet, they have grown apart. The classical college before the War between the States was largely an adjunct of religious institutions. After that war, the modern college and university came into being under the leadership of strong presidents and strong boards of trustees with many members drawn from industry, banking, and agriculture, and from the legal profession that served all three. Thorstein Veblen[3] exaggerated the situation, but there was some truth to his complaint that the captains of industry and of finance ruled the universities through what he called the "Captains of Erudition" (the presidents).

This has changed. Faculty members began asserting their influence, particularly at the end of World War I, and their power has grown more or less continuously. In the 1960s, students began accumulating more influence as they became a larger and more active market force within higher education,[4] and they even gained some power in governance, at least temporarily, through mass protests. But, perhaps of greatest importance, state control has been increasing with glacial persistence, driving on almost unchecked. The comparative influence of trustees as a consequence has declined, and fewer trustees are drawn from industry. The corporation and the college are much less managed by interlocking directorates than they once were.

The corporation and the university are growing apart in other ways. The corporation has been particularly attracted by the "investment in people" aspects of higher education. Yet more attention is now paid by some students to the consumer aspects of college attendance—to enjoyment of the college experience as a "slice of life," and to preparation for the cultural components of postcollege life. Also, the purpose of higher education least liked by industry—dissent—is now ranked higher in the hierarchy of campus goals than in earlier times and is likely to remain there for the indefinite future. Intellectuals, centering their lives on campus, are more numerous than ever before, more protected by academic and other freedoms, and, in a postindustrial society, more critical of some aspects of industrial activity (such as exploitation of the environment). They constitute the chief component of what Lionel Trilling called the "adversary culture."[5]

Although the college and the corporation are increasingly separate in their identities, they are also more dependent on each other. Higher education draws on the wealth created in large part by and through industry—it draws 2.5 percent of the GNP. Higher education depends on industry for many of the jobs for its graduates. It also depends on the benevolence of industry, as well as of other segments of society, for a significant portion of its income and some of its freedom from domination by the state. No longer is the church the main support of the college, as it was for over two centuries; now it is a pluralistic industrialized society that provides the support.

The corporation, in turn, is increasingly dependent on the university for research and skilled personnel. Most basic research takes place on campus. Furthermore, the campus conducts the great talent hunt for industry. Both are done with substantial success. This is now a "knowledge society"; the "knowledge industry" is at the center of growth and change, and the campus is at the center of the knowledge segment of society. This will become ever more the situation. No reversal is likely or, perhaps, even possible. Fritz Machlup once calculated that "knowledge production" and distribution (very broadly defined) constituted almost 30 percent of the GNP.[6]

Thus the corporate world has both less influence but more dependence on the university world than ever before. And the college world, in turn, has more intellectual independence from corporate leadership but more resource dependence on industrial production. The two worlds are more separate in their identities, yet more dependent on each other in the conduct of their activities; more suspicious of each other, yet more bound to each other for mutual survival; more apart in philosophical purposes, and more together in mundane practice.

Some facts:

Trustees drawn from industry and business constitute about 40 percent of all trustees of American colleges and universities.[7] This percentage varies enormously, however, from institution to institution—nearly 100 percent at MIT to nearly 0 percent in some theological seminaries.

Industry and business, through gifts, grants, and contracts, supply about 3 percent of the funding of colleges and universities.

Industry and business absorb about 50 percent of the graduates of colleges and universities.

To the statement "The board is too subservient to special interests in the community," negative replies constitute the following percentages:[8]

Board chairs	96 percent
Presidents	90 percent
Faculty leaders	81 percent

and to the statement that the board "provides freedom of teaching and research for faculty," positive replies constitute the following percentages:

Board chairs	94 percent
Presidents	93 percent
Faculty leaders	83 percent

The University-Industry Axis

The close contacts with industry through direct financial support and through indirect influences within the political processes, while not controlling, are, as I have observed them, consequential:

• Drawing academic activity toward favored areas, such as business administration and engineering, and in earlier times agriculture, and away from

the liberal arts; and, more generally, away from what Martin Trow has
called the "autonomous functions"[9]
- Within research, drawing activity in more applied directions
- Generally, aiding larger more than smaller establishments
- Creating, overall, a disproportionate distribution of societal support within
  higher education in favor of (a) technologically oriented research universities and (b) labor-market-responsive four-year comprehensive colleges and
  two-year community colleges versus other types of institutions
- Diverting thought, time, and energy from teaching and basic research to
  more entrepreneurial activities by some faculty members, thus also creating
  a two-class professoriate of higher-income entrepreneurial-academics as
  against less-well-remunerated academic-academics
- Capturing, by individual companies, of first access to some new discoveries, and giving special favors to cooperative faculty members in return
- Tempting faculty members to use academic facilities for private gain
- More generally, promoting opportunistic, as against academic, mentalities
  in the professoriate, and encouraging the emergence of a netherworld of
  pseudo-intellectual activity
- Occasionally supporting efforts to directly influence the "ideology" of academic institutions—only very occasionally successfully
- Indirectly increasing the proportion of students and faculty in the more politically "safe" areas of the campus, such as engineering and business administration, and reducing the counter culture areas, such as sociology
- Drawing academic institutions, as the result of one or another of the above
  impacts, into public controversies, such as over the greater support to agri-
  business than to the family farm

These impacts, some of them potentially or actually negative, are, on
balance, in my judgment, more than offset by these positive advantages:

- Adding additional funds to higher education directly from industry and indirectly by support of public funding
- Encouraging substantial contributions by higher education to economic
  growth generally, and to specific industries and areas
- Aiding greater contact by academics with the realities of the productive activities of society
- Engendering greater public support for higher education as beneficial to
  economic and social advance, including job creation

Dangers that some social critics predicted would result from an industry-
university alliance have not come to pass: by Thorstein Veblen that the "Captains of Industry" would increasingly dominate the "Captains of Erudition";
by Abraham Flexner[10] that there would be a degradation of the academic

spirit; and by many Marxists that the potentially transformational contributions of higher education would be totally subjugated to the dominant repro-
ductive functions.[11]

There have been individual abuses rather than any general subversion of
the academic ethic. MIT and Cal Tech have not sold their souls to the devil.
What Faustian bargains have been made are more by institutions of lesser
stature and particularly by certain segments of, and faculty members within,
them—also of lesser stature.

Industry has never exerted the influence and control over related aspects
of academic life that was exerted in past times by the ancient professions of
theology, medicine, and law in their respective areas of concern. I have been
impressed, as I have served on boards of trustees of institutions of higher education and foundations, by how carefully trustees from the corporate world
have nearly universally separated their corporate interests from their trusteeship responsibilities. Conflicts of interest are against the law, and even more
against the moral standards of the groups involved, which enforce them con-
scientiously. Also, trustees have loyalties to their colleges and universities
that are quite separate from any corporate connections they may have. The
corporation and the college are treated as worlds apart.

The role of industry needs to be put in perspective. It is a source, as
noted above, through grants and contracts and gifts, of less than 3 percent of
all income of institutions of higher education; but this 3 percent is quite un-
evenly distributed, creating potentially significant leverage in some areas in
some institutions. This industry support is divided almost equally between
private and public institutions. Corporate influence is exerted more in three
indirect ways: (1) through the student market as students seek to prepare for
the corporate world; (2) through governmental R&D and other funding agencies as they reflect the interests of industry and agriculture; and (3) through
faculty contacts via consultancies. It is mostly through these mechanisms that
any imbalance toward corporate interests comes about, and not through trusteeship and direct financial support as the less sophisticated and more idco-
logical critics allege.

Suggestions

What can be done, if anything, to maintain or improve cooperation in
this essential but tension filled relationship between the university and the
corporation?

First, the college must protect its hard-won independence. But it should
exercise its independence according to some reasonable rules of conduct, and
there have been violations of such rules in recent times. Examples of such
rules include these: to rely on persuasion, not on confrontation and violence,
both on campus and off, in advancing political causes; to rely on academic

merit in appointments and promotions of faculty members and in student advancement, not on ideology; to rely, to the maximum extent possible, on factual objectivity and balanced analyses in teaching, not on attempted indoctrination; and to refrain from using the campus, as an institution, for individual economic aggrandizement.

The college, also, should not turn its back on advancing human capability. This purpose is sometimes viewed as crass materialism and abject service to society. But better research and higher skills, while sometimes leading to greater profits or more military power, also lead to better health, more education, better citizenship, higher culture—a higher quality of life for more people.

Additionally, the college should be careful not to assert too strongly, or believe too deeply in, the "moral superiority" of the academic community above all other groups of people, and not to make excessive claims of wisdom for "the intellectual" far removed from responsibility.[12]

Second, the corporation should seek to understand that the academic world is different. It lies politically, for one thing, to the left of the American public generally. For example, a 1975–76 Carnegie Commission survey found that 30 percent of faculty members agreed with the statement "Meaningful social change cannot be achieved through traditional American politics."[13] But it should also be emphasized that 70 percent disagreed. The professoriate, it should be noted, is more dispersed from right to left than any other group in society. It is far from monolithic. This is inevitable, given the nature of intellectuals. The corporate world, by contrast, is generally to the right of the American public and much more internally conforming in its thinking. So long as the rules of conduct are reasonable and are followed, the differing inherent natures of the academic world and the corporate world should be both mutually understood and tolerated.

The corporate world should also seek to understand students, particularly in a youth-oriented society. They are often at the cutting edge of history. After the burning of a Bank of America branch in Isla Vista, Louis Lundborg, former chairman of the board of Bank of America, went to visit with students. His reactions moved from "righteous indignation" to an understanding of a "new value system" being born.[14] There is much to be learned from students, despite their volatility.

The corporate world also should continue its support of higher education generally, not insisting on ideological support in return. I have disagreed on this point with David Packard—otherwise a long-time and effective friend of higher education. He has noted that boards of trustees have less control over their colleges than they once did and are more mixed in their memberships, and that faculty members now have more control and are often led by a "militant minority." In addition, he has said that universities are sometimes a "haven for radicals who want to destroy the free enterprise system," and that many students have been taught to be "anti-business." Consequently, he has suggested targeting contributions so that corporate "dollars are constructive rather than destructive." For example, he has advised, in giving funds, to "restrict them to areas you believe are educating the right kind of professors."[15]

It is understandable how corporations might be more interested in supporting the advancement of human capability rather than political dissension; but a policy of picking and choosing departments, projects, and professors to support on the grounds of contributions "to the general welfare of our free enterprise system" and of seeking to penalize those who are "hostile to business" would be difficult to define and potentially dangerous to apply. One consequence of such action is that it is likely to be detrimental to the acceptance on the individual campus and in the academic world of those agencies or individuals selected as friendly. And most important, such action would enhance the tendency toward politicization and polarization on campus—a tendency to be resisted from whatever direction it comes. In any event, corporations have little leverage, since they supply such a small percentage of the funds for higher education, and the attitudes of the vast majority of scholars cannot be bought for money.

Rather, corporate support should be general in nature, although perhaps more for the purposes of advancing human capability than for others. But it should not be subject to political tests, and it should go, perhaps even disproportionately, to what Packard calls the "bell cow" universities even though the orientation of their faculty members and students is the more liberal. Furthermore, corporations, for the long-run welfare of the nation, should be supportive of the funding of colleges and universities by other sources, particularly by the state and federal governments. It is a good investment in the future.

Some tension is inevitable, even desirable, provided it occurs within reasonable rules of conduct. This is a pluralistic society with many centers of power and influence, the corporation and the university prominent among them. Such a society, for its preservation and its progress, requires joint efforts at understanding—by keeping "in touch," exhibiting a modicum of tolerance all around, and recognizing the need for some restraint. It also requires an appreciation of the conditions for mutual survival now that the corporation is so dependent on the life of the mind, and the college on the resources and the freedom accorded to it by society.

Rules of Conduct

As the corporate-university connection intensifies, it becomes more important to make explicit rules of conduct that will guide it. My suggestions follow.

To the corporate world:

Do not seek to politicize academic life by insisting on a pro-business ideology.

Do not unbalance higher education unduly in favor of applied fields.

To the university world:

Defend academic freedom, institutional autonomy, and principles of balance among intellectual fields.

Insist that faculty members owe their basic loyalty to the university—to their teaching and their research and to time spent on the processes of institutional governance, and thus that they not neglect their teaching and research and their citizenship responsibilities in governing academic life.

Require that faculty members make known their contracts and other affiliations with industry, and that they not use university facilities, without compensation to the university, in order to serve industry.

Require that any research done on university time and with university facilities be openly published, and not made available on a secret basis to one or another component of industry.

Balance service among large and small competitors (for example, in agriculture, between agricultural "factories" and family farms), and as between opposing elements, such as industry and labor.

Maintain an unbiased commitment to the pursuit of truth.

The biggest danger areas, as I see them, in university-corporation contacts are as follows:

• Where one segment of an industry is favored over another, or the interests of producers are favored over those of consumers, or there are other imbalances
• Where, formally or informally, first access or even exclusive access to new knowledge is given to a sponsoring company versus its competitors, where university resources are used for this purpose[16]

Knowledge was once for its own sake (Socrates); then it was also for power (Bacon); now it is also for money. Money is not the source of all evil, but it is the source of some; eternal vigilance may not be the sole antidote, but it is one.

Notes

This chapter is based on a presentation I made to the International Forum for Higher Education in Tokyo in September 1989, sponsored by the International Council on Educational Development and the Association of Private Universities in Japan. It also draws on a speech delivered at "Business Tomorrow: The University and the Corporation Conference" in Chicago, 18 November 1973 (*California Management Review* 16, no. 3 [Spring 1974]: 20–24); copyright 1974 by the Regents of the University of California, portions reprinted by permission of the Regents.)

1. Other individual illustrations of strong cooperation are the Tata Institute in Bombay, the University of Minerals and Technology in Dhahran, and the Bucconi School of Management in Milan.

2. See, in particular, Upton Sinclair, *The Goose-Step: A Study of American Education* (New York: AMS Press, 1970); originally published in 1923.

3. Thorstein Veblen, *Higher Learning in America* (Stanford, Calif.: Academic Reprints, 1954); first published in 1918.

4. See the discussion in David Riesman, *On Higher Education: The Academic Enterprise in an Era of Rising Student Consumerism* (San Francisco: Jossey-Bass, 1980).

5. Lionel Trilling, *Beyond Culture: Essays on Literature and Learning* (New York: Viking Press, 1965).

6. Fritz Machlup, *The Production and Distribution of Knowledge in the United States* (Princeton: Princeton University Press, 1962), 362.

7. *Chronicle of Higher Education* 31, no. 22 (12 February 1986): 27, table.

8. Clark Kerr and Marian L. Gade, *The Guardians: Boards of Trustees of American Colleges and Universities* (Washington, D.C.: Association of Governing Boards of Colleges & Universities, 1989), tables B-2, B-1.

9. Martin Trow, "Reflections on the Transition from Mass to Universal Higher Education," *Daedalus* 99, no. 1 (1970).

10. See the discussion in Abraham Flexner, *Universities: American, English, German* (New York: Oxford University Press, 1930).

11. See the discussion in Sheila Slaughter, *The Higher Learning and High Technology: Dynamics of Higher Education Policy Formation* (Albany: State University of New York Press, 1990).

12. John T. Dunlop, "The Cambridge-Washington-Cambridge Commute" (Talk given to the Harvard Club of Washington, D.C., 25 October 1973).

13. *Carnegie Council National Surveys 1975–76*, vol. 2, *Faculty Marginals*, Question 51M (Berkeley: Carnegie Council on Policy Studies in Higher Education, 1978).

14. Louis B. Lundborg, *Future without Shock* (New York: Norton, 1974), 20, 28.

15. David Packard, *Corporate Support of Private Universities* (New York: Committee for Corporate Support of American Universities, 1973).

16. A particularly sensitive issue is where such exclusive access is accorded a foreign corporation (as has happened), and public funds have been used. To subsidize foreign competition is bound to be suspect. At a minimum, care should be exercised in the calculation of full overhead charges.

CHAPTER 6

The Decline of the American Economy I:
Is Education Guilty or Not?

This essay may be viewed by some as an act of treason! It says that American education, including higher education, was not primarily guilty (superficially convincing evidence to the contrary) of initiating the recent comparative decline of the United States economy. I say, on the contrary, that "seldom in the course of policy making in the United States have such firm conclusions rested on so little convincing proof."

The audience at the University of Minnesota, where this presentation was made, was at best skeptical at first; and a few members were irate, in subsequent discussions, that I should advance this line of argument—regardless of how correct it might be.

My evaluation, that education is subject to too much blame, and to too-high expectations and too soon, goes against much current wisdom. It also goes against the wishes of many defenders of American industry and of governmental policies that want a scapegoat to deflect responsibility away from those they seek to protect. It also goes against the wishes of much of the educational establishment that hopes to be found guilty so that education may be given more money to improve itself substantially. It should be given more money with the hope, but not the assured expectation, that it will improve itself, and for other reasons than just contributions to the economy.

In the area of the economy, I find, as others have also, an overall rough balance currently (the future is more problematical) between what the labor market needs and what education in its several forms provides. There are, however, some existing specific deficits to which I call attention and where improvement is essential and even urgent. Also, any major deterioration in the schools from present levels due to current budgetary problems or other sources would certainly cause damage to the economy in the longer run. Further, some parts of the labor force will need higher skills to meet the demands of the future—but I think that education (and particularly at the college level) is potentially able to provide these higher skills, given the resources and effective policies. I see, instead, more intransigent long-term problems on the labor-market side than on the schooling side of the demand-supply equation: The quality of jobs, for perhaps a quarter of the labor force, is deteriorating, and sometimes severely. Supply in the labor market generally follows demand, and we currently have more problems on the demand than on the supply side. And it may be noted that "surplus schooling" can have a negative effect on productivity by increasing job dissatisfaction and turnover.[1]

It is my view that there are important shorter term supply problems in terms of the education of workers but that they can be overcome as so spectacularly demonstrated in World War II, but that there are even more important longer term demand problems in terms of quantity and quality of jobs as shown so spectacularly in the Great Depression. We need to look hard also at the demand side.

Education is an imprecise word to use, for education is not a single entity. A central theme of this essay is that there are three sources of education that roughly evenly impact preparation for the labor market: (1) the family, (2) the schools, and (3) on-the-job training and supervision. What is often called "education" is really only "schooling," and this distinction should be clearly made and is made in what follows. The use of the job as an educational instrument in the United States is clearly inferior to its use in Germany and Japan and some other industrial nations. The schooling system is of more problematical impact— often inferior at the primary and secondary levels but usually superior at the higher education level. In evaluating "education," we must look at all three major institutions and not just at "schooling" alone, and within "schooling" at the separate levels

Of central importance: Education should serve society in a balanced way and not concentrate so exclusively on economic growth.

The responsibility that has been placed upon schooling, including within higher education, for the comparative decline in the U.S. economy is, in my judgment, as I shall seek to show below, excessive.[2] A report prepared for the National Science Foundation by the National Governors' Association and the Conference Board concludes: "Education [schooling] was viewed by all three groups—business, academia, and government—as the key to the nation's competitiveness."[3]

Schooling is certainly to some degree a key, but it shares responsibility at least with (1) government policies affecting savings, investments, R&D expenditures, budget deficits, foreign trade deficits, poverty, and poor maintenance of the economic infrastructure, including roads, among other items; (2) business policies and attitudes including those affecting capital investment, R&D, on-the-job training, respect for and fairness toward the work force, quality of products, again, among many other factors; and (3) family attitudes and conduct affecting composition of the family and attention to education at home. We need across-the-board examinations of the many problems in their totality and from a long-run point of view.[4]

One consequence of seeking to make schooling *the* key to competitiveness, in addition to placing too much responsibility on the schools, may be to neglect the other elements of the complex set of causations and solutions within the tangled web. But there are also three additional negative consequences: (a) external forces will try to control schools too much; (b) in the process, schools may become too unbalanced in the direction of economic contributions alone; and (c) failures to meet heightened expectations will result in subsequent too great recriminations.

The central theme of this essay is that, in improving economic performance, yes, schools are a factor, but, no, schools are not the only or the main factor. A secondary theme is that schools serve the economy but not only the economy. We need a more balanced view both of the causes of the current distressed economic situation and of the solutions, and of the several roles of schools in society. The pursuit of schooling is not alone for the sake of the pursuit of wealth.

I make these comments with some hesitation. The current attention to schools as the major source of economic decline, even if largely misplaced, may have many good side effects in raising teachers' salaries, in reducing class sizes, in expanding Head Start, in lengthening the hours per year devoted per pupil to educational activities, in bringing teachers and parents more into the decision-making process, and in many other ways. This attention to schools also has the encouraging impact of demonstrating public interest in and support for them. But the potential harm to society, and to schooling itself, in neglecting more important sources of decline, it seems to me, outweighs the potential advantages in concentrating attention so heavily on schools, for which, in any event, there are other, better arguments.

The better arguments for improving schools are these:[5]

1. It takes knowledge to be a good citizen in a very complex society and in a world with many problems.
2. It takes skills to cope with everyday life—paying the income tax, taking care of personal health, educating children, and so much else.
3. Schools are important in advancing greater equality of opportunity.
4. Schooling is essential to advancing participation in the cultural life of the nation.

TABLE 5

Annual Rates of Gross Domestic Product Growth per Worker, Selected Countries, 1951–1987

Country	1951–60 (%)	1961–73 (%)	1974–79 (%)	1980–87 (%)
United States	2.0	1.9[a]	0.0[b]	0.8
Canada	2.4	2.6	1.3	1.0
Japan	6.5	8.2	2.9	2.8
France	4.4	4.9	2.7	1.9
West Germany	5.7	4.1	2.9	1.5
Italy	5.7	5.8	1.7	1.9
United Kingdom	2.1	2.9	1.3	1.8

Source: Barry P. Bosworth and Robert Z. Lawrence, "America in the World Economy," *Brookings Review* 7, no. 1 (Winter 1988/89): 44. (The authors note the use of unpublished data from the Department of Labor, the Bureau of Labor Statistics, and the Office of Productivity and Technology.)

[a]This is a period with two quite contrary performance records:

1961	3.5	1969	0.3
1962	3.6	1970	0.9
1963	4.0		
1964	4.4		
1965	3.0		
1966	2.9		
1967	2.9		
1968	3.0		
1971	3.2		
1972	3.0		
1973	2.3		

[b]The rate in 1974 was −1.9 (*Economic Report of the President, 1990* [Washington, D.C.: U.S. Government Printing Office, 1990], Table C-47.)

About three-fourths of the jobs in the United States take less knowledge and fewer skills than being a good citizen or coping with daily life.

Causes for Concern over the Potential Negative Impacts of Schooling on the Economy

Why all this attention to the economy? The answer is, of course, clear: It is not performing well. Output per work hour has fallen from an average increase of 2 percent per year in the long run (1870 to 1930),[6] and sometimes 3 percent or more during the two decades after World War II, to about 1 percent more recently, and in some years none at all. Among advanced industrial nations, our performance is the worst. (See table 5.) For seventy years (1920–

TABLE 6

Youth Unemployment Rates, 1986

	Teenagers[a]	Young adults[b]
United States	17.7	10.1
White	15.6	8.7
Black	39.3	24.1
Canada	16.8	14.3
Japan[c]	4.8	
France	33.6	21.1
West Germany	6.4	7.9
Italy	41.8	29.8
United Kingdom	20.8	17.0

Sources: International data: Organisation for Economic Co-operation and Development, *OECD Employment Outlook* (Paris: OECD, 1988), table 2.6.
Racial groups in the United States: Calculated from U.S. Bureau of the Census, *Statistical Abstract of the United States: 1988*, 108th ed. (Washington, D.C.: U.S. Government Printing Office, 1987), table 611.

[a]Ages 14–19 for Italy; 16–19 in the United Kingdom and United States; 15–19 in all other countries.
[b]Data refer to persons 20–24 years of age.
[c]Data refer to youths aged 15–24.

90) the American economy has been dominant in the world. Suddenly it may be in the process of losing this position,[7] and the nation is shocked. And the United States, along with other nations, finds it particularly difficult to integrate youth into the labor market in making the crucial transition from schools to employment. (See table 6.)

Why all this attention to the role of schools? To begin with, Americans have great faith in schools as a solution to problems, and great advances have been made historically.[8] On the surface, also, it may appear that schools can actually provide substantial solutions to the special problem of the health of the economy. "Education" has been estimated, as will be noted below, to be the source of 20 percent of the increase in national income per person employed over the approximately fifty-year period from 1929 to 1982; and "advances in knowledge" account for an additional 40 percent, or a total of 60 percent. Without closer examination, this would appear to be quite conclusive "proof" that education, including research, is so heavily involved in advances in the economy that it is the most likely suspect when those advances falter.

Additionally, it seems often to be considered that the schooling system is particularly subject to change; otherwise why all the many reports on how to change it? Governors, in particular, are likely to concentrate on schools. Schools are largely a state responsibility, and the quality of schooling facilities may help to redistribute employment opportunities among the states, as the electronic industries in Massachusetts and California once benefitted from the high quality of their universities, even though schools may not add so decisively to the productivity of the nation as a whole.

Schooling and the Initiation of the Decline in Productivity Growth

What "proof" is advanced that schools might be guilty? Declines in College Board Scholastic Aptitude Test scores (verbal and mathematical) prior to the declines in productivity increases are the main "proof."[9] Productivity changes, with a lag of two to four years, do parallel changes in test scores to an amazing, almost eerie, degree (see figure 1). This suggests that productivity followed schooling.[10] There is at least one other possible explanation (aside from pure chance), which is that both trends responded to other developments that had similar consequences on each—I shall return to this possibility later (chapter 7). The public at large and policymakers in particular seem to have accepted the implications of the patterns displayed in figure 2 without much question because the other evidence that came to them—much of it anecdotal—also indicated that the schools had deteriorated, and they were predisposed, in any event, to view education as a fundamental basis for the conduct of all of American society.

The horrendous error in trying to explain the changes in productivity by changes in SAT scores, whether up or down, is the short time lag, sometimes two years, sometimes four years. Only about half of the high school graduation-age cohort has entered the labor force after two, and even after four, years, because of continuing education in college, entry into the military forces, and unemployment. Thus, even after four years, only about 5 percent of the employed labor force will have been affected (assuming an average labor force participation of forty years), and this mostly the least-skilled segment and thus least responsible for productivity. And half the drop in SAT scores has been found (see note 10) to be due to a drop in the aptitude of the more numerous test takers as the nation moved rapidly from mass to universal access to college.

There is no way that a relatively minor decline in test scores (cumulative rates eventually of 5 to 10 percent for mathematical and verbal, respectively) for 5 percent of the labor force could possibly explain any major percentage of the decline in the rate of productivity increases based on the performance of the total labor force! What appears to justify the argument that changes in SAT scores caused changes in rates of productivity increase is the rapid sequential parallel rates of changes. In fact, the fast response utterly destroys the argument, since the alleged cause could not possibly have had the alleged effect in that short a period of time. *Post hoc* in this case cannot be *ergo propter hoc.*

FIGURE 1

**Patterns of Change in Annual Rates of Productivity Increases and in
Combined SAT Scores, 1960 to Late 1980s**

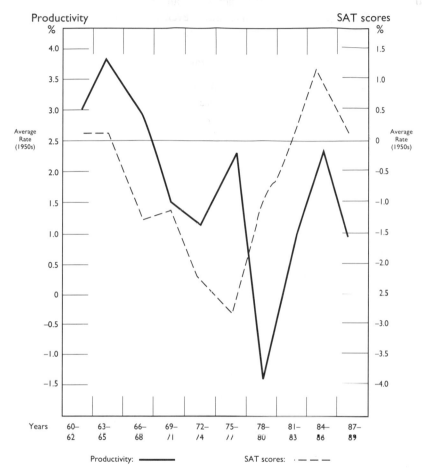

It might, also on an equally simplistic *post hoc* basis, be said that the rise
in M.B.A. degrees conferred per year was a cause of the decline in the rate
of productivity increases. Productivity increases slumped from their historic
levels beginning about 1970, and 1970 starts a period when M.B.A. degrees
more than doubled: from 26,500 in 1970–71 to 69,500 in 1987–88! *Ergo
propter hoc?*

The *Nation's Report Card* scores, contrary to the SAT scores, show generally steady scores over the period of time covered by both sets of
evaluations.[11] These "report cards" show achievement more than aptitude
(as in the Scholastic *Aptitude* Tests), and the schools are more responsible for

FIGURE 2

SAT Verbal Scores of High School Graduates, and GRE Verbal Scores of College Graduates, 1965–1989

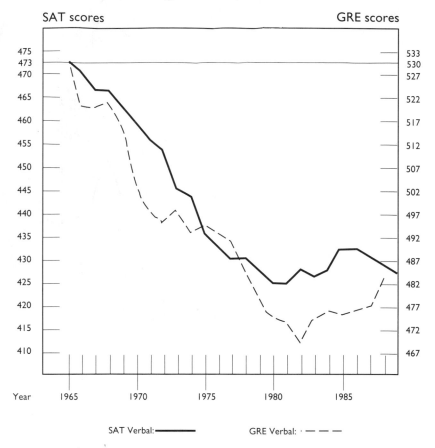

SAT Verbal:━━━━━   GRE Verbal: · — — —

achievement than for aptitude. This is to argue not that these "report card" score levels are adequate—for they are not—but only that they do not indicate declines in school performance.

It strikes me as absurd, after a deeper examination of the evidence, that so much blame is placed on declining SAT scores for the comparative decline of the American economy. Seldom in the course of policy making in the United States have such firm conclusions rested on so little convincing proof.

Test scores out of college tell a different story. Verbal scores show the same patterns (see figure 2). Mathematical scores show the same early decline but then a remarkable improvement to above historical levels (figure 3). The full range of test scores out of college shows a mixed situation (table 7).

FIGURE 3

SAT Mathematical Scores of High School Graduates, and GRE Quantitative Scores of College Graduates, 1965–1989

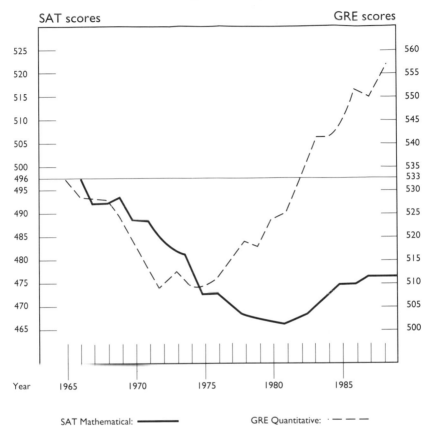

More scores (15) have gone down than have stayed even or increased (9), but those in the latter group are generally more associated with productivity (for example, GRE Math) than those in the former (for example, GRE Sociology).

Overall it can be said that (1) higher education has made up for some of the deficiencies in prior education, in other words, that it has increased its "value added," and (2) it has done better in improving mathematical than verbal skills.

It should be noted that social justice, as well as economic effectiveness, is an issue. We concentrate many more resources on some levels of the labor force than on others. Perhaps half or more of lifetime investment in training

TABLE 7

Differential Changes in Test Scores Out of College, 1965–1982

Degree of Change in Score	Test
Moderate increase	LSAT (1975–82)
	GRE Math
Small increase	MCAT Biology
	GRE Physics
No change	LSAT (1968–74)
	MCAT Chemistry
	GRE Quantitative
	GRE Biology
	GRE Economics
Small decline	GMAT (1965–82)
	MCAT Reading
	GRE Chemistry
Moderate decline	MCAT Quantitative
	GRE Geology
	GRE Music
	GRE Engineering
	GRE Psychology
	GRE Education
Large decline	GRE Verbal
	GRE History
	GRE English Literature
	GRE French
Extreme decline	GRE Political Science
	GRE Sociology

Source: Based on Clifford Adelman, *The Standardized Test Scores of College Graduates, 1964–1982* (Washington, D.C.: National Institute of Education, 1985), table C.

Underlined subjects have the closest ties to production functions.

at school plus on-the-job is concentrated on those with a college education and thus on one-quarter of the total work force. This investment might be 45 percent currently, while an earlier estimate was 60 percent for United States males in 1958.[12] For some estimates, see table 8.

The Comparative Economic Role of Schooling in Advancing Productivity

What overall contributions the formal schooling system makes to the productive activities of American society is a very difficult question to answer with any precision. I shall try to indicate answers to it in broad terms

TABLE 8

Comparative Educational Investments in Segments of the Labor Force

	Approximate Levels of Education of Total Labor Force	Very Rough Estimates of Educational Investments in School and on the Job[a]
College educated	25 percent	45 percent
Post-high-school educated (community colleges, vo-tech schools, military)	25 percent	25 percent
High school educated	25 percent	17 percent
Less than high school educated	25 percent	13 percent

[a]Based on the assumption that investment in on-the-job education is roughly proportional to in-school education. Family contributions almost certainly vary even more than instruction in school and on-the-job by level of family and education.

only, recognizing room for disagreement, and I shall rely, principally on, among other authorities, Edward F. Denison of the Brookings Institution.[13] I shall be seeking only indications of possible general orders of magnitude.

Our specific concern centers on Denison's evaluation of the contributions of (1) "education" and of (2) "advances in knowledge" to the growth rate of actual national income for the whole economy during the 1929 to 1982 period *on the basis of per person employed*. Contributions per person employed are what basically determine the overall advances in real wages, and thus in the standard of living, and thus also in the base from which per-capita taxes are paid. What is not produced cannot be consumed or otherwise expended on a long-run basis. Calculating from Denison's data,[14] first taking out negative contributions, such as fewer hours worked per employed person—and these are substantial (35 percentage points)—we find that positive contributions over the period 1929–82 were divided as follows:

Education per worker	20 percent
Capital per worker	15 percent
Advances in knowledge	40 percent
Improved resource allocation	12 percent
Economies of scale	13 percent
	100 percent

These allocations, viewed simplistically, put a heavy burden on education—apparently some responsibility, taken together, for the 60 percent represented by education per worker and by advances in knowledge.

There are, however, some important qualifications necessary to these estimates by Denison.[15] "Education" is measured by years of schooling. It is not possible from Denison's data to separate out, as one would wish to, either education (1) within the family or (2) via on-the-job training, or the comparative contributions of the several levels of in-school training—it is a lump-sum category of "education."[16] It may be noted, however, that greater in-school training is usually matched by greater on-the-job training, since workers with more formal education are more likely to be in employment where more on-the-job training is given and over a longer period of time. In-school training has a double impact: first in its own right, and then second in sorting out those persons judged potentially more responsive to on-the-job training, who then obtain the jobs that involve more such training.

About one-third of the contributions to output per worker through "education" beyond the family level is by education on the job[17]—roughly one-third of educational investment is in on-the-job training, and the rate of return is roughly the same as to more formal education. No one knows how to divide the other two-thirds among education in elementary, secondary, tertiary, and post-tertiary formal education; nor how to assign responsibility to the family, which might be the most important of all.[18]

The family has almost certainly deteriorated the most as an educational institution. The family contributes to education in several important ways, including through

- Preschool—the amount and quality of instruction in reading and writing and the consequent effects on early and, to some extent, continuing performance in school
- In-school—the degree and direction of influence on work habits, including TV viewing and concentration on homework
- Postschool—the impact of encouragement and support to continue education at the postsecondary level

Education starts in, and highly depends on, the conduct of the family.

Employers apparently have more responsibility (one-third) within the category of post family education than is generally realized. I note, in passing, the success of Germany with its apprenticeship system. I also note the success of Japan with its excellent secondary system, particularly in mathematics, and with on-the-job training. In the United States, each level of formal education has played an essential but relatively modest role in the growth of income per person employed; but the United States is distinguished among nations by a particularly effective system of higher education. It should also be noted, more generally, that segments of education may substitute for each other, and that one nation may rely more on one segment and another on another: for instance, Germany relies more on apprenticeships, Japan on secondary education and on-the-job training, and the United States on higher education. The best solution among nations is to make the best use of all approaches. The next best solution is to choose the approach with the highest payoff. The United States has done that—concentrating on the one-quarter of the labor force that comprises about half of accumulated skill training.

It is important to note also, in looking at the contribution of education to productivity:

A nation may advance rapidly in productivity without a significant rise in schooling attainment of the work force. It has been estimated that, in the period from 1950 to 1962, the schooling impact, by raising the quality of labor, contributed 25 percent to rising national income per person employed in the United States but only 3 percent in West Germany, where many less-educated foreign workers came to be employed.[19]

The United States is sending work abroad to nations, such as Mexico, to be done by less-educated workers than those displaced in the United States. This is done, presumably, not for the sake of gaining access to a more highly schooled labor force, and, thus, not because of failures in the American schooling system.

Summary of Observations from the Evidence[20]

1. Productivity increase declines followed SAT score declines by about two to four years, but, at that latter point, only about 5 percent of the labor force could have been affected, and this could not include those with the most advanced skills out of college.
2. One-half of the decline in SAT scores has been ascribed to the changing composition of the test takers as larger proportions of the age cohort began attending college;[21] and SAT tests do not, in any event, cover most high school students—mostly only those who plan to go on to college, and not all of them. Also, the *Nation's Report Card* scores show a generally steady series of results.
3. Verbal SAT scores went down by about 10 percent at the low point (figure 3), and mathematical by about 5 percent (figure 4). (Note that language skills are particularly taught in the family and mathematical within the schools.) Productivity increases, however, at their low point totally collapsed to zero.
4. "Value added" increased at the level of higher education in the especially important mathematical area, and came to more than offset the declines out of high school. About half of total investment in training is concentrated on those who attend college, and they come out of their college years overall nearly even with historical levels. And graduate training within U.S. higher education is generally considered among the best in the world.

FIGURE 4

High School Graduation Rates, 1968–1985[a]

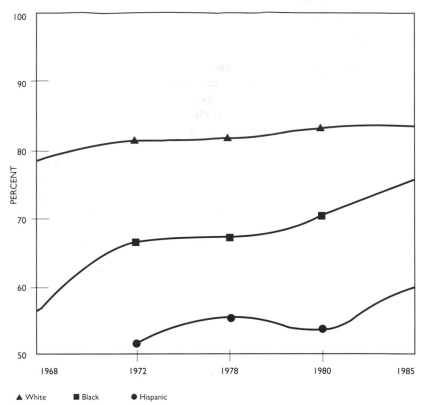

▲ White   ■ Black   ● Hispanic

Source: James R. Mingle, *Focus on Minorities: Trends in Higher Education Partici-pation and Success* (Denver: Education Commission of the States and the State Higher Education Executive Officers, 1987), 4. (Based on U.S. Bureau of the Census, *Current Population Reports,* ser. P-20. no. 404 and no. 409.)

[a]Percentage of the 18 to 24-year-old population with four years of high school.

5. One-third of postfamily investment in training takes place on the job, and an unknown percentage of the total in the family. Whatever blame there is due to declining contributions of "education," "schooling" within education must share it with these other two sources.

6. High school graduation rates have increased slightly. The greater quan-tity of graduates, even if they are of lesser quality (figure 4), helps to offset declining SAT scores out of high school. And higher proportions of high school graduates go on to college.

7. In any event, "education" (as measured) has borne only around one-fifth of the responsibility for changes in rates of productivity growth in the United States.

I also note:

8. The rates of productivity increases went down all over the highly industrialized world and at about the same rate: by one half. The declines in productivity growth, in terms of gross domestic product per worker hour, fell from 4.5 percent per year (1956–73) to 2.2 percent (1973–86) in OECD countries, on the average, and from 2.4 to 1.2 percent in the United States.[22] Something more must have been at work other than a deterioration of the formal schooling system in the United States.

9. Japanese-managed firms in the United States (about five hundred of them) generally report that they obtain the same levels of output and quality of work from American workers as they do in Japan from Japanese workers—as, for example, in the production of the Honda Accord.

10. Manufacturing productivity rose 3.5 percent per year in the 1980s in the United States using the same labor force as did the total economy; and the United States, within manufacturing, has had the best record with those highly competitive industries based on advanced technology, which are the industries most in need of well-educated workers. James K. Galbraith concludes that "in the industries where the U.S. remains highly competitive, there is just no evidence of a labor problem."[23]

I conclude that (1) the primary and secondary schools, net, are a minor key to the decline of the American economy;[24] (2) training within higher education, net, is more a key to positive improvements than to negative results; and (3) the more important explanations must be found elsewhere.[25] Formal schooling in the United States has been subject to more blame for the slowdown in productivity than can be justified; to higher expectations for near-term future contributions to an improved economy than can be met; and, increasingly, to a single test of performance, which can distort the composition of its total contributions to society.

Notes

This chapter is based on the George Seltzer Distinguished Lecture I presented at the University of Minnesota, 10 October 1989.

1. See Mun C. Tsang, Russell W. Rumberger, and Henry M. Levin, "The Impact of Surplus Schooling on Worker Productivity," *Industrial Relations* 30, no. 2

(Spring 1991): 209–28. ("One solution to the widespread concern that the U.S. is losing its competitive edge in the international marketplace has been to increase the quantity and quality of workers' schooling. The study suggests that such action may be ineffective at best and counterproductive at worst" [226].) It may well be true that "more than half of our young people leave school without the knowledge or foundation required to find and hold a good job" (U.S. Department of Labor, *What Work Requires of School*, June 1991). It is also true that many of the jobs available to young people are not "good."

2. As it is also in the judgment of Lawrence Cremin, who commented that "to contend that problems of international competitiveness can be solved by educational reform, especially educational reform defined as school reform, is not merely utopian and millennialist, it is at best foolish and at worse a crass effort to direct attention away from those truly responsible for doing something about competitiveness and to lay the burden instead on the schools" (Lawrence Cremin, *Popular Education and Its Discontents* [New York: Harper & Row, 1990], 103). See also the observations by Harold Howe II in "Commentary," *Education Week*, 12 December 1990; and Lawrence Mishel and Ruy A. Teixeira, *The Myth of the Coming Labor Shortage* (Washington, D.C.: Economic Policy Institute, 1990).

3. The National Governors' Association and the Conference Board for the National Science Foundation, *The Role of Science and Technology in Economic Competitiveness* (Washington, D.C.: National Governors' Association, 1987), 1. See, additionally, the discussion in Commission on Workforce Quality and Labor Market Efficiency, *Investing in People* (Washington, D.C.: U.S. Department of Labor, September 1989); also the Public Agenda Foundation and the Kettering Foundation, *Regaining the Competitive Edge* (Dayton: National Issues Forum Institute, 1990); and many other similar reports.

4. For excellent such approaches, see Michael L. Dertouzos, Richard K. Lester, and Robert M. Solow, *Made in America* (Cambridge, Mass.: MIT Press, 1989); William J. Baumol, Sue Anne Batey Blackman, and Edward N. Wolff, *Productivity and American Leadership: The Long View,* (Cambridge, Mass.: MIT Press, 1989); and Michael E. Porter, *The Competitive Advantage of Nations* (New York: Free Press, 1990).

5. The Carnegie Council on Adolescent Development particularly stresses emphasis on education (1) for responsible citizenship and (2) for healthful lifestyles. (*Turning Points: Preparing America's Youth for the Twenty-first Century* [New York: Carnegie Corporation of New York, 1989]). See also Diane Ravitch and Chester E. Finn, Jr., *What Do Our Seventeen-Year-Olds Know?* (New York: Harper & Row, 1987) for a discussion of what seventeen-year-olds do not know in the areas of history (affecting citizenship) and literature (affecting cultural participation).

6. Baumol, Blackman, and Wolff, *Productivity and American Leadership,* 70.

7. The United Kingdom lost its dominant position beginning in 1890 when a "1 percentage point lag in productivity growth" transformed it "from the world's undisputed industrial leader into the third-rate economy it is today" (Ibid., 2).

8. In the short period since 1950, for example, the proportion of the adult population that has a high school diploma has doubled, and the proportion with a college degree has tripled—enormous accomplishments.

9. American College Testing scores have also gone down and up roughly in parallel.

10. For other discussions of the relation of SAT scores to productivity, see Martin Neil Baily, who, for the period 1968 to 1979, rejected a decline in test scores out of high school as a "major cause of the productivity slowdown" and found that at most it explained "a small fraction of the slowdown." Baily found a much stronger explanation in the quality of new entrants into the labor force during that period of time, as many young workers and women entered the labor force with low levels of on-the-job training. He noted that "productivity growth will improve as young workers and women acquire experience and age," and this seems to be one of the explanations for the rise in the 1980s. Baily also notes that one-half of the decline in the SAT scores can be explained by the higher proportion of young people taking the tests, some of them with less adequate preparation. (Martin Neil Baily, "Productivity and the Services of Capital and Labor," *Brookings Papers on Economic Activity,* no. 1 [1981]: 1–50.) See also Baily, "What Has Happened to Productivity Growth," *Science* 234, no. 4775 (24 October 1986), where he concludes that declining SAT scores had "only a minor productivity effect." However, it has been suggested that, over a longer period of time, the deterioration may have had a more significant cumulative impact on the quality of the total labor force. John H. Bishop, by 1987, finds a substantial impact. He calculates that if improvements in test scores had continued at the rate from 1942 to 1962, rather than deteriorating, then there would have been a very major favorable impact on productivity. He calculates a loss of 1.25 grade level equivalents in educational content after 1967 to 1986 per high school graduate. "General intellectual achievement" has declined significantly, and this will affect the labor force for a long time to come, even if test scores should return to earlier levels. "The major impact on productivity growth has come in the 1980s" and by then had become an "important drag on productivity growth." (John H. Bishop, "Is the Test Score Decline Responsible for the Productivity Growth Decline?" *American Economic Review* 79, no. 1 [March 1989]: 178–97.) I note, however, that the great decline in productivity growth took place before "the major impact" in the 1980s is said to have occurred, and thus other explanations must be given for the origins of that great decline.

11. An examination of the series of studies identified as *The Nation's Report Card* (A program of National Assessment of Educational Progress conducted by the Educational Testing Service) results in a different view of the situation. Instead of scores fluctuating down and up, they show a more steady situation than do SAT scores. This seems to me to be a much more likely correct reading of the situation than rapidly fluctuating scores implying rapidly fluctuating performances by the schools. Schools do not change that much, that fast, in their performances. Trends are shown for 1971 to 1988 covering assessments of performance of nine-year-olds, thirteen-year-olds and seventeen-year-olds in reading, and in each case they show slight improvements. Trends are shown from 1974 to 1988 in writing at grade 4, grade 8, and grade 11, and they show "substantially" no change. Trends in mathematics are shown

from 1972 to 1987 for ages nine, twelve, and seventeen, and they show slight improvements overall. Trends for science are also shown for the same years and age groups and, all ages taken together, show roughly no change but a decline at age seventeen. Trends in civics from 1976 to 1988 show a slight decline for age group seventeen. *Report Cards* on history and geography were prepared only for 1988 and thus show no trend lines. At a minimum, these "report cards" imply no changes in school performance as a possible source of declines or increases in productivity, but their starting points are after the decline in productivity increases already had set in. (See U.S. Department of Education, *Accelerating Academic Achievement*, 1990, fig. 2.2. See also Educational Testing Service, *The Education Reform Decade* (Princeton: Educational Testing Service, 1990), 12; and their *Performance at the Top* (1990).

12. Calculated from Jacob Mincer, "On-the-Job Training Costs, Returns, and Some Implications," *Journal of Political Economy* 70, Supplement (October 1962): table 1. For a current study of the "learning industry" with its heavy concentration on technical workers, managers, and professionals, see Nell Eurich, *The Learning Industry* (Princeton: Carnegie Foundation for the Advancement of Teaching, 1991). It is estimated that formal training by industry affects as much as one-third of the nation's work force. The Magaziner-Brock-Marshall Report (Commission on the Skills of the American Workforce [Ira C. Magaziner, William E. Brock, and Ray Marshall, Cochairs], *America's Choice* [Rochester, N.Y.: National Center on Education and the Economy, 1990]) finds that two-thirds of company training dollars are spent on those with a college education. I note that on-the-job training has two major components— the formal, specially scheduled training, which can be counted, and the informal, which takes many forms and cannot. The informal comes in more casual instructions and suggestions by supervisors, in comments by fellow workers, in observations of how others do their work, in reading instructions and manuals, and in trial and error.

13. See, in particular, Edward F. Denison, "The Interruption of Productivity Growth in the United States, *The Economic Journal* 93, no. 369 (March 1983): 56–77; and idem, *Trends in American Economic Growth, 1929–1982* (Washington, D.C.: Brookings Institution, 1985).

14. Denison, *Trends in American Economic Growth*, p. 30.

15. The Denison estimates are only one set of several. For instance, in "Measuring the Impact of Education on Productivity," Mark Plant and Finis Welch have estimated the "contribution of increased stock of education" to "growth in productivity" at 26 percent in *Education and Economic Productivity*, ed. Edwin Dean [Cambridge: Ballinger, 1984], 188); and Larry L. Leslie and Paul T. Brinkman, after a careful review of the literature, say that "the percentage of national income growth deriving from education and higher education, respectively, are estimated to be 15–20 and 4–5 percent, with another 20–40 percent probably deriving from improvements in knowledge and its applications" (*The Economic Value of Higher Education* [New York: Macmillan, for the American Council on Education, 1988], 21). Robert M. Solow attributes a figure as high as 60 percent to advances in knowledge ("Growth Theory and After," *American Economic Review* 78, no. 3 [June 1988]: 307–17).

16. Lawrence Cremin has noted "the impossibility of even comprehending the processes and effects of schooling . . . apart from their embedment in a larger ecol-

ogy of education that includes what families, television broadcasters, workplaces, and a host of other institutions are contributing at any given time" (*Popular Education and Its Discontents,* viii.)

17. Mincer, "On-the-Job Training," 50–79. (See also Jacob Mincer, *Schooling, Experience, and Earnings* [New York: National Bureau of Economic Research, 1974].) In his original study (1962), Mincer came up with a figure of one-third to one-half of educational contributions as due to on-the-job training. In a more recent study, however, he comes out with a figure of one-third, which is the figure I shall use (Jacob Mincer, *Costs of Returns and Wage Profiles,* Technical Paper no. 12, National Center of Education and Employment, Columbia University, 1989.) This distribution of one-third to on-the-job training seems reasonable to me. Beyond the ability to read, write, and do simple arithmetic, all "educational" contributions to productivity are on-the-job for many and even most positions in the American economy—I estimate about one-half. Formal education makes the greatest contributions in the categories of professional, technical, and administrative occupations, which comprise about one-quarter of the American employed work force; informal education, including instruction on-the-job, makes a greater contribution to performance for many of the other three-quarters. The Mincer estimate, which he calls "very tentative," cannot be said to have been fully proven, but it has not, to my knowledge, been "falsified"—to use the famous phrase of Karl Popper. For a recent survey by Mincer of literature on the continuing high returns to on-the-job training and the large amounts of such training, see Jacob Mincer, "Human Capital and the Labor Market," *Educational Researcher* 18, no. 4 (May 1989): 27–34. For a discussion of the importance of "company training" to increasing earnings, see also Lee A. Lillard and Hong W. Tan of the Rand Corporation, *Private Sector Training: Who gets It and What are Its Effects,* (Santa Monica, CA: Rand 1986). For an analysis of the impact of education on wage premiums in "educational intensive industries" (including finance, medical, and professional services), see Kevin Murphy and Finis Welch, "Wage Premiums of College Graduates," *Educational Researcher* 18, no. 4 (May 1989): 17–26.

18. Ravitch and Finn (*What Do Our Seventeen-Year-Olds Know*) find that "proficiency" of students most closely relates to parental education and "a literate home environment," but is also strongly influenced by time spent on homework, by television viewing per day, and by school attendance patterns—all of which are impacted by the family. They find that "tracking" (general, academic, vocational) also affects proficiencies, but, on the average, they find few differences among students attending public schools (on an academic track), Catholic schools, and other private schools (see chap. 3). See also the observations of L. Scott Miller that "the variations in family resources are much larger than the variations in school resources" ("A Long Deep View of Minority Improvement," *American Association for Higher Education Bulletin* 43, no. 8 [April 1991]: 3–7). See also the comment that "parental involvement in a child's education is a crucial factor in promoting academic achievement" Donald A. Rock, Judith M. Pollack, and Ann Hafner, *The Tested Achievement of the National Education Longitudinal Study of 1988 Eighth Grade Class* (Washington, D.C.: U.S. Department of Education, Office of Educational Research and Improvement, [1991]). It is also generally true that students who start ahead on entering schooling not only stay ahead but get farther ahead as they go along.

19. Edward F. Denison, *Why Growth Rates Differ* (Washington, D.C.: Brookings Institution, 1967), 299, 309. See also the discussion on the use of foreign labor in Charles P. Kindleberger, *Europe's Postwar Growth* (Cambridge: Harvard University Press, 1967).

20. Sar A. Levitan and Frank Gallo (*Got to Learn to Earn: Preparing Americans for Work,* Occasional Paper 1991-3 [Washington, D.C.: Center for Social Policy Studies, George Washington University, September 1991]) come to many of the same conclusions as the summary below. They say that "contrary to periodic alarms, supply shortages in particular occupations occur rarely, and are much less troublesome than the opposite problem of unemployment" (31). They also note that "the means of organizing work may be as important as the quality of the workforce. The industrial revolution, which brought about the first major historical upsurge in productivity, preceded the rise of mass education. Although Japan and Germany, the two other largest industrial democracies, have narrowed the productivity gap between themselves and America, the U.S. lead remains large. . . U.S. productivity is almost twice that of Japan's (100 vs. 58) if the comparisons are adjusted for hours worked" (16).

21. See Baily (note 10 above). See also Harold Howe II, "SAT Score Decline" (*Phi Delta Kappan* 66, no. 9 [May 1985]: 599–602), for a review of the evidence that "51 percent of the decline in verbal scores and 56 percent of the decline in mathematical scores" was due to "changes in the test-taking group"; and for other non-school sources of the decline. He concludes that "it makes sense to blame about half of the score decline on significant changes in the composition of the test-taking group, about one-quarter of the decline on school-related factors, and about one-quarter of the decline on broader social factors." See also Brian Powell and Lala Carr Steelman, "Variations in State SAT Performance," *Harvard Educational Review* 54, no. 4 (November 1984): 389–412.

22. See Angus Maddison, *The World Economy in the Twenty-first Century* (Paris: OECD, 1989), table 7.2.

23. James K. Galbraith, "A New Picture of the American Economy," *The American Prospect,* no. 7 (Fall 1991).

24. For a similar conclusion, that it is "not true" that "the deterioration of America's schools has been a significant cause of the drop in the productivity growth rate," see Richard J. Murnane, "Education and the Productivity of the American Work Force," in *American Living Standards: Threats and Challenges,* ed. Robert E. Litan, Robert Z. Lawrence, and Charles W. Schultze (Washington, D.C.: Brookings Institution, 1988).

25. I agree with Lester Salamon that "the connection between investments in human capital and improvements in output and economic performance may be far less direct in practice than it appears in theory"; there are many "complications." (Lester Salamon, "Overview: Why Human Capital? Why Now?" in *Human Capital and America's Future,* ed. David W. Hornbeck and Lester M. Salamon [Baltimore: Johns Hopkins Press, 1991], 6.)

CHAPTER 7

The Decline of the American Economy II:
Who Then Is Guilty, and Are There Solutions?

This chapter follows on the discussion in the prior chapter and is taken from the same source—both chapters with revisions. Chapter 6 says that schooling is not more than marginally responsible for the recent comparative decline in the American economy. Who then is guilty? The answer given here is, nearly everybody. And who can provide solutions? Again, nearly everybody.

We talk of "labor productivity." This actually is a complex concept. It involves the contributions to productivity from all sources, which are then divided by worker hours or worker years. It is not just the productivity of the labor force as affected by, among other factors, the knowledge, skill, and habits of work of the employed members of the labor force. It also involves the contributions of managerial policies and competence, capital investment, new technology, the changing quality and quantity of resources, the policies of government, and much else. We are actually talking about total *factor productivity, as measured against inputs of labor. In terms of credit or blame or responsibility for deteriorations or improvements, we must think in terms of managerial productivity and societal productivity,[1] and also family productivity as well as labor force productivity.*

There are currently problems with labor force productivity in the United States, including, particularly, (1) clerical offices with high school graduates who have, in fact, only an eighth-grade education, (2) skilled crafts with too little in the way of apprenticeship training, (3) high-quality precision work done by workers with low-quality habits of work, (4) new models of teamwork but too few people with the needed skills for self-management and quality control, and (5) fast-changing technologies but too few people with a highly developed ability to learn new skills, including reading and writing complex manuals and blueprints. There are these specific problem areas affecting a minority of the labor force. But there is no overall shortage of training and skills in the American labor force, and particularly not of training and skills due to deficiencies in schooling alone.

There are also many problems with managerial productivity, including the ability to give effective leadership to the labor force. And there are many problems with societal productivity, including government policy affecting savings and investment, and the amount and distribution of research and development funds; and with family productivity in terms of contributions to habits of work, aspirations and motivation, and preparation to enter school.

Figure 2, in chapter 6, nevertheless, still remains a puzzle: Allowing for a two- or four-year lag, why did changes in productivity increases so parallel the prior changes in SAT scores? As we have shown in the prior chapter, it is highly unlikely that the latter were a major cause of the former. At best, the case for a verdict of "guilty" against schooling in general, and higher schooling in particular, has not been clearly proven; at worst, it has not been proven to any significant degree.

It may be speculated that one common cause may have been the great "counterculture revolution" of the 1960s, which affected behavior in many spheres of society, including much of the labor force, with its emphasis on self-gratification (including drugs and alcohol), rejection of rules and authority, and the downgrading of merit as a basis for advancement. Each of these aspects would almost equally affect both schooling and the total labor force, and together they could add up to a very major impact. Also, the counterculture revolution ran out of steam, and there were counterreactions that had taken hold by the 1980s, when both test scores and productivity started to rise again. The counterculture revolution, it may also be noted, was a phenomenon around the world in the OECD nations, within all of which rates of growth in productivity went down by about half.[2]

It should be quickly added, however, that the counterculture revolution has had its positive aspects as well, which, among other things, could serve to improve education and productivity in the longer run, including more opportunities for women and minorities, and more concern for preservation of the environment.

Two good possibilities, subject to more proof, as to why productivity went down and then up are the OPEC oil crises, which made energy first more and then less costly, and the introduction of vast numbers of new workers (women and youth) into the labor force, first reducing productivity and then increasing it as "human capital" was accumulated through on-the-job training. But there seem to be no similarly good explanations for the course of SAT scores, except that, once they went down, greater efforts were made to raise them. But why did they go down so much in the first place? A new generation of additional test takers, as noted earlier, may be half of the explanation, and the counterculture revolution could account for some of the other half.[3]

What Went Wrong?

One way of looking at the problem of the comparative decay of the American economy is from the vantage point of what went wrong. Much did, but, according to Denison, not the contribution of "education" overall in the period after 1973 to 1982 when the real trouble with productivity became fully evident (1974 was the worst year). Only "education" and "weather in farming," among all factors, according to his calculations, continued their positive contributions to increasing productivity.

In all of this, it should be emphasized, we are working with what is measurable. Denison finds much that is not separately measurable but potentially important, including among his "miscellaneous determinants":

• How hard workers work
• How well managers manage

He suggests that the latter of these two factors has been a much more likely source of decline in productivity growth than the former, and I agree: "It is plausible, if not demonstrable, that, one way or the other, much of the decline in residual productivity is traceable to management."[4] This is also the burden of the argument in the MIT study *Made in America*.[5] Those who once claimed so much of the credit when all went well must accept some of the responsibility when all seems to go wrong: American management—its policies and its conduct. If there is such a thing as *the* key, I find it here more than in schooling.[6] However, as Denison has said, "everything may have gone wrong."[7]

It may be noted, nevertheless, that management has probably more total responsibility for changes in productivity than does any other segment of American society:

• Major responsibility for education via training on the job
• Major responsibility for advances in knowledge via R&D (industry spends 72 percent of all R&D funds), for transfers of new knowledge into production, and for failures in the area of Denison's "miscellaneous determinants"
• Major responsibility for capital investment within the framework of federal economic policies[8]

Management performance, federal policies (including on R&D), the American family, and American society each deserves at least as much consideration in explaining the comparative decline of the American economy as do the schools and the colleges; and the schools and colleges deserve at least as much consideration for their citizenship and consumption functions as they do for their production functions. To the extent that guilt can be assigned, it rests more with those who overemphasize the role of schooling in the decline of the economy and who, as a consequence, also overemphasize the production functions of schooling.

Overall, however, much that is potentially important cannot be measured, and much that can be measured cannot be disaggregated in ways that are helpful in formulating policy. The contributions of econometrics are useful only to a modest degree in solving the most important of all American economic problems.[9] The one big message of econometrics, however, is the importance of advances in knowledge.

Where Do the Productivity Problems in Schooling Lie?

They do not lie generally in an overall "skills shortage." The most authoritative study to date, the Magaziner-Brock-Marshall report, says that "with some exceptions, the education and skill levels of American workers roughly match the demands of their jobs."[10] Actually they show, if anything, a surplus of education for economic purposes. They conclude that 34 percent of the labor force does not need more than eight years of education for the jobs they hold, yet 94 percent of the U.S. population has completed at least that level. Another 36 percent of jobs, they find, require eight to ten years of education and some additional job-focused training. The other 30 percent require sixteen years of education or more —about equaling the current supply. The "some exceptions" include certain clerical occupations and craft trades. They find that only 15 percent of all employers report difficulty in finding workers with appropriate occupational skills.[11]

My own conclusions, from a reading of many studies and from long personal experience, and particularly as the chairman for the last fifteen years of the Work in America Institute with tripartite participation including national leaders in industry and organized labor, are slightly different. I would divide the labor force into four major segments of about equal proportions:

About one-quarter of all jobs (farm and other laborers, service workers, unskilled operators) require an ability to follow verbal instructions and competence in the most basic mathematical skills, and this requires less than a four-year high school education. Good work habits are the most important asset here.

About one-quarter (skilled operators and lower-level sales and clerical personnel) require the additional ability to follow increasingly complex written instructions and to keep simple records, and this usually requires a high school education.

About one-quarter (technicians of many sorts, skilled craftsmen, and higher-level clerical personnel) require additional specialized skills attained in some formal training on the job, apprenticeships, post-high-school schooling, and military service.

About one-quarter require advanced knowledge and skills (administrators, professionals, high-level technicians) obtained in four years of college and beyond.

This distribution is roughly paralleled by the actual education of the American labor force—about one-quarter do not complete high school, about one-quarter complete high school and obtain no further formal training, about one-quarter add additional formal training below a four-year college degree, and about one-quarter obtain college degrees and advanced degrees. As I see it, general problems for the first of the above four quarters are with motivation and work habits; the second with basic verbal and mathematical skills; the third with adequate applied training; and the fourth with assured continuing expansion of opportunities.

The biggest specific educational deficiencies, as I see them, are in the clerical occupations that require a full high school education, but where many students actually perform at an eighth- or tenth-grade level in basic verbal and mathematical skills, affecting institutions like banks and insurance companies, and in craft trades—and this is in line with the Magaziner-Brock-Marshall report. Also in line with that report is the conclusion that what is most needed, beyond basic skills, are better work habits: more employees who are "reliable, steady and willing to follow directions," and with a "good work ethic," which is the area where "80 percent of employers" express their "primary concerns."

The above deficiencies are the areas where, on a comparative basis with Japan and Germany as our major competitors, our labor force is least competitive. Several developments make these deficiencies even more troublesome for the future: (1) the greater and greater emphasis on quality of work, (2) the spreading use of the computer in workplaces, (3) the increasing complexity of instructional manuals, and (4) the decentralization of decision making to work-level groups.

With respect to current labor markets, however, and broadly generalizing, I do not find the American worker to be either "overeducated"[12] or "undereducated" to any major degree. The schooling system and the choices by students and their parents have generally been quite responsive to the labor force needs of society. I worry less about "poor workers" than about "poor jobs," because the supply side is more amenable to constructive solutions than the demand side. The American population, however, it appears to me, is clearly "undereducated" for good citizenship, for coping with increasingly complicated lives, for full equality of opportunity, and for advancing cultural participation.

What Can Be Done?

The future will be different from the past. This discussion has been mostly concerned with whether or not schooling, in any major way, has in the recent past injured the performance of the economy. The sequential question, regardless of the answer to the prior question, is: How might it best aid performance in the future? This future holds two contrary developments: (1) a need for many workers with lesser skills in the expanding service trades—and this holds many perils; and (2) a need for higher skills in the new technology sectors in response to what the Magaziner-Brock-Marshall report calls the "third industrial revolution." [13] The upskilling problem is easier to handle via the schooling system, which is quite responsive, than is the deskilling problem—what happens to people in the deskilled segment of the economy? And they may involve about equal numbers of workers. Aside from upskilling, schooling can assist workers in adjusting to new and better ways of working, particularly via decentralization of responsibilities to work teams and individuals. Modest but important improvements, via schooling, are possible and can be useful. [14]

My suggestions follow: [15]

Outside formal schooling:

Pay more attention to education in the family. The family may be the most important school of all. [16]

Put more emphasis on preschool training, as in Head Start. Only 20 percent of potentially eligible children living in poverty are now included.

Pay more attention to the quality of on-the-job training.

Primary and secondary schooling:

Pay more attention to basic skills. Try to assure that a twelve-year degree represents at least a ten-year education, including by the use of achievement tests whose results might accompany the high school diploma—as an incentive for better performance. Also, allow young people to return to school easily and at no cost to them in order to raise the level of their achievement test scores.

Put more emphasis on good habits of work, which are instilled by, among other sources, classroom experience. [17]

Increase the number of hours per year spent by students in the classroom and on homework assignments. [18]

Improve the retention rates to completion of a degree in high school. [19]

Consider giving the high schools, as in Sweden, responsibility for placing their graduates, whether in jobs or in advanced forms of education.

Even with the best of policies and performances, however, there are strict limits to what can be expected from the schools in improving the performance of the economy. The schools operate in an unfavorable environment of deterioration of families, of competition with commercial video and audio for student attention, and of the many attractions of street life.[20] Also, any improvements in student schooling levels will take at least ten years to show up in changing the qualifications of a significant segment of the total labor force.

Higher education, if it wants to, can more easily achieve improvements than can the schools.

Higher education:

Improve transfer programs from community colleges to four-year institutions.

Improve remedial work in use-of-language skills.

Greatly expand community college programs to aid and advise young persons generally in the advancement of their lives and careers.[21]

Increase the opportunities for women and underserved minorities to achieve advanced degrees.

Put more emphasis, in schools of business administration and engineering, on production-level skills; and in schools of education on all forms of education and not only on "schooling." In general, I believe that the greatest single trend in the reorientation of program efforts within American higher education, as already in Western Europe, will (and should) be toward more emphasis on training polytechnic type skills and toward more polytechnic type applied research and technology transfer. This is where the competitive battles will focus increased attention.

The states:

Assist educational and other institutions in the above efforts.

Greatly improve U.S. transition-to-work programs, which the Magaziner-Brock-Marshall report calls the worst in any advanced industrial country.[22]

Federal government:

Greater support for Head Start.

Greater support for Pell grants. The nation loses about 10 percent of its best talent because of lack of a college education, mostly due to lack of family resources. Underserved minorities are most affected.

More expenditures on nondefense R&D, which is 1.7 percent of GNP in the United States, 2.6 percent in the former West Germany, and 2.8 percent in Japan.[23]

Increase national R&D funds spent through the universities. These are now 14 percent, while the general range for several advanced industrial nations (Australia, Canada, France, Italy, Japan, Norway, Sweden, and West Germany—with the exception of the United Kingdom, which is at about 12 percent) is 15 to 30 percent.[24] Higher education, it should be noted, is responsible not only directly for the proportion of R&D funds it spends but also indirectly for the education of the scientists and engineers employed by the other suppliers of R&D funds; and the R&D funds it spends are disproportionately weighted toward basic research. Thus higher education is central to "advances in knowledge."

Less attention within federal R&D on research in the military area and in the health of the out-of-the-workforce aged (over 60 percent of federal R&D is in the military area, as against under 5 percent in Japan; and 12 percent in the health area, as against a range elsewhere of 2 to 4 percent); and more attention to "industrial development," which receives 15 percent of the total in West Germany and under 1 percent in the United States.[25]

More attention in university research to applied research and to the transfer of research results into production improvements.

Changes in federal R&D programs in particular provide both the best leverage, through contributions to "advances in knowledge," and the quickest possible returns.

Regardless of how much emphasis is placed on the economic roles of schooling, there are other highly important roles to consider:[26]

1. Preparation for good citizenship. This also requires, as a minimum, a high school education and constant self-education after high school.
2. Preparation for coping effectively with life off the job—handling personal finances, personal and family health, high-quality consumption and investment decisions, interpersonal relations. This also requires, at a minimum, a high school education and constant efforts at self-improvement.
3. Advancement of equality of opportunity.
4. Advancement of cultural understanding and participation.

The nation desperately needs a better schooling system for several reasons, but because there are several reasons, it needs a system that is not solely directed to any one of these reasons, including service to the economy.

The United States, for many reasons and not alone its schooling system, is trashing significant segments of an entire generation of youth.[27] Thus the current emphasis on improving schooling, provided it is a balanced approach, is well worth the current attention—for the nation is "at risk" in several educational dimensions.[28] But remedial action is also necessary in many other aspects of American life and not just in schooling alone—American society, as a whole, is "guilty."

Notes

This chapter is an excerpt from my "Education and the Decline of the American Economy: Guilty or Not?" the George Seltzer Distinguished Lecture delivered at the University of Minnesota, 10 October 1989.

1. For an indication of how important "societal productivity" may be, see the discussion in Abram Bergson, "The USSR Before the Fall: How Poor and Why," *Journal of Economic Perspectives* 5, no. 4 (Fall 1991): 29–43. "Even after due allowance for differences in labor quality, and in capital and land per worker . . . output per worker in the USSR is 27–37 percent below that among OECD countries" (43).

2. A somewhat related explanation might be called the "decline of capitalism" hypothesis (or, perhaps better, the "decline of industrialism" hypothesis, for communist nations were also affected at about the same time). It is argued that "job satisfaction" has gone down and that there has been a "rising cost of keeping people down"—the need for more supervision, for more quality control, for more plant security; and that a decline in "work intensity" is a major cause of the slowdown in productivity. (See Samuel Bowles, David M. Gordon, and Thomas L. Weiskoff, *After the Waste Land: A Democratic Economics for the Year 2000* [Armonk, N.Y.: M. E. Sharpe, 1991].)

3. See the discussion in Advisory Panel on the Scholastic Aptitude Test Score Decline, Willard Wirtz (Chairman), *On Further Examination* (New York: College Entrance Examination Board, 1977). The report notes that the prior decade had been a "decade of distractions," including a major increase in TV viewing by young persons—high school students now spend five hours on watching TV to one hour on homework.

4. Edward F. Denison, *Trends in American Growth, 1929–1982* (Washington, D.C.: Brookings Institution, 1985), 40–41. For a more qualified conclusion that an "underemphasized" reason for the slowdown in productivity "may be found in managerial practices" but that "the evidence is not definitive," see Martin Neil Baily and Margaret M. Blair, "Productivity and American Management," in *American Living Standards: Threats and Challenges*, ed. Robert E. Litan, Robert Z. Lawrence, and Charles W. Schultze (Washington, D.C.: Brookings Institution, 1988), 193, 214.

5. Michael E. Dertouzos, Richard K. Lester, and Robert M. Solow, *Made in America* (Cambridge: MIT Press, 1989).

6. This is also the conclusion of William J. Baumol, Sue Anne Batey Blackman, and Edward N. Wolff (*Productivity and American Leadership: A Long View* [Cambridge: MIT Press, 1989]). They emphasize as causes of decline problems in the areas of investment, R&D, entrepreneurship, and technology transfer, in particular, but they also note the shift of employment to service industries, where increases in productivity are harder to achieve, and growing scarcities of natural resources; and, within education, poor educational results for disadvantaged minorities. (See particularly chap. 12.) For a discussion of how "slow innovation" may have been a major cause of the productivity "slow down," see Martin Neil Baily and Alok K. Chakrabarti, *Innovation and the Productivity Crisis* (Washington, D.C.: Brookings Institution, 1988). See also Frederich M. Scherer, "The World Productivity Growth Slump," in *Organizing Industrial Development,* ed. Rolf Wolff (Berlin: Walter De Gruyter, 1986).

7. Edward F. Denison, "The Interruption of Productivity Growth in the United States," *The Economic Journal* 93, no. 369 (March 1983): 56–77.

8. For an emphasis on the importance of capital investment, see D. W. Jorgenson, F. M. Gollup, and B. Fraumeni, *Productivity and U.S. Economic Growth* (Cambridge: Harvard University Press, 1987). " . . . the contribution of capital input [was] the most significant source of growth [for 1948–79]" (20).

9. For a discussion of some of the substantial and differing literature on education and output, and of the many technical problems in analysis, see Richard B. Freeman, "Demand for Education," in *Handbook of Labor Economics,* vol. 1, ed. Orley Ashenfelter and Richard Layard (Amsterdam: North Holland, 1986).

10. Commission on the Skills of the American Workforce (Ira C. Magaziner, William E. Brock, and Ray Marshall, CoChairs), *America's Choice* (Rochester, N.Y.: National Center on Education and the Economy, 1990), 28.

11. Ibid., 25. For a discussion of recent studies that conclude that there is "a rough equilibrium between the education of the workers and the demands of their jobs," see Laura D'Andrea Tyson, "Failing Our Youth," *New Perspectives Quarterly* 7, no. 4 (Fall 1990): 26–30.

12. See Richard B. Freeman for a conclusion that "overeducation . . . has existed in the labor market for some time" (*The Overeducated American* [New York: Academic Press, 1976]). See also Russell W. Rumberger, *Overeducation in the U.S. Labor Market* (New York: Praeger, 1981), 97. For a contrary view, see Jacob Mincer, "Comment: Overeducation or Undereducation," in *Education and Economic Activity,* ed. Edwin Dean (Cambridge, Mass.: Ballinger, 1984).

13. "Jobs near the middle of the male distribution have disappeared" (Gary Burtlees, *A Future of Lousy Jobs?* [Washington, D.C.: Brookings Institution, 1990]). For a summary and discussion of the literature on downskilling and upskilling, see Kenneth I. Spencer, "The Upgrading and Downgrading of Occupations," *Review of Educational Research* 55, no. 2 (Summer 1985): 125–54. For the "striking" finding of a "pronounced slowdown," in the period 1960 to 1985, in the rate of growth of skill requirements of jobs in the American economy, see David R. Howell and Edward N. Wolff, "Trends in the Growth and Distribution of Skills in the U.S. Workplace,

1960–1985," *Industrial and Labor Relations Review* 44, no. 3 (April 1991): 486–502. For a discussion of prospective future changes in the composition of jobs, see Anthony Patrick Carnevale, *America in the New Economy* (Washington, D.C.: U.S. Department of Labor, 1991). "Cognitive skill" requirements have risen the most, and this is the area where the United States, via postsecondary education, may have a competitive advantage.

14. I do not find it persuasive to say that "more than half of our young people leave school without the knowledge or foundation to find and hold a good job" (Secretary's Commission on Achieving Necessary Skills [William H. Brock, Chairman], *What Work Requires of Schools* [Washington, D.C.: U.S. Department of Labor, 1991]). Aside from calling attention to the unsolved problem of defining a good job, it may be noted that it could, perhaps, equally be said that one half of all jobs are not good jobs and there is no point in acting as though all jobs are good jobs and advising that all young people should be trained on the assumption that they are.

15. A technical paper for the MIT *Made in America* study finds the greatest weaknesses in the American education system in relation to productivity to be (1) inadequate on-the-job training, (2) deficiencies in basic skills, and (3) chaotic arrangements for transition from school to work. The second of these weaknesses particularly relates to the schools. (See Richard Kazis, "Education and Training in the United States," in *The Working Papers of the MIT Commission on Industrial Productivity,* vol. 2 [Cambridge: MIT Press, 1989].)

16. See, for example, the Work in America Institute project now in progress on using the workplace to assist parents to educate their children.

17. In earlier times, children were usually introduced to patterns of work within the family on the farm or in family-level service or craft enterprise. In recent times no substitutes have been provided for this experience. I consider that this change is at least as important as what has happened inside the classroom. Employers particularly want (1) conscientious attendance, (2) a sense of responsibility for the quality and quality of work output, (3) ability to cooperate with co-workers, and (4) willingness to accept supervision. (For an excellent list of "employability skills," see Employability Skills Task Force, *Progress Report* of the Michigan State Board of Education [October 1989].)

18. For a discussion of the importance of time spent, see Ernest L. Boyer, *High School: A Report on Secondary Education in America* (Princeton: Carnegie Foundation for the Advancement of Teaching, 1983). For a more cautionary view that, while more student time does increase educational achievement, it may not be the most cost-effective method, see Henry M. Levin and Mun C. Tsang, "The Economics of Student Time," *The Economics of Education Review* 6, no. 4 (1987). American children engage in about two-thirds as many hours of educational activity as Japanese children (Bonnie Gordon, "Cultural Comparisons of Schooling," *Educational Researcher* 16, no. 6 [August-September 1987]), 4–7.

19. Employers are interested in the diploma itself because it is an indication of persistence in pursuit of goals and an at least minimal willingness to accept discipline.

20. José Ortega y Gasset once wrote (in *The Mission of the University* [London: Kegan Paul, 1946], 38; first published in 1930) that "the school depends far more on the atmosphere of national culture in which it is immersed than it does on the pedagogical atmosphere created artificially within it." I agree. In the United States, the schools have been, like King Lear, more "sinned against than sinning."

21. See the discussion in Carnegie Council on Policy Studies in Higher Education, *Giving Youth a Better Chance* (San Francisco: Jossey-Bass, 1979).

22. See also Educational Testing Service, *From School to Work*, Policy Information Report (Princeton: Educational Testing Service, 1990).

23. National Science Foundation, *National Patterns of R&D Resources: 1989*, (NSF 89-308, table B-19. See also National Science Foundation, *International Science and Technology Data Update: 1988*, National Science Foundation Special Report NSF 89-307 (Washington, D.C., 1988), 8.

24. *UNESCO Statistical Yearbook, 1990*.

25. National Science Foundation, *National Patterns of R&D Resources: 1989*, NSF 89-308.

26. See also the discussion by Howard R. Bowen, who once wrote that the "potential incremental return [of "widening" and "deepening" higher education] will be mainly in the fulfillment of individual lives and the building of a humane civilization rather than in raising the earnings and status of individuals and in augmenting the gross national product" (Howard R. Bowen, *Investment in Learning* [San Francisco: Jossey-Bass, 1977], 457).

27. See Harold Howe II, "Thinking about *The Forgotten Half*," *Teachers College Record* 92, no. 2 (Winter 1990): 293–305, for an excellent list of suggestions on how to assist disadvantaged youth. He draws on the reports of the Grant Foundation, *The Forgotten Half* (Washington, D.C., January 1988 and November 1988).

28. The National Commission on Excellence in Education, *A Nation at Risk: The Imperative for Educational Reform* (Washington, D.C.: U.S. Government Printing Office, April 1983).

PART III

The 1990s and Beyond:
Some Special Perplexities

Introduction: A Mince Pie

The future is always problematical. Among foreseen forces, there are usually several in uncertain contention. Then there is the possibility—and almost the certainty, in changing times—of unforeseen developments. And how society, institutions, and individuals react to the prospects they see in advance, and to any surprises that may come along, have their impacts, too. As E. B. White once said, "The future . . . seems to me no unified dream but is mince pie." And we all want to be in on the baking.

The chapters that follow are about the baking of the "mince pie" of the 1990s and beyond. There will be an even greater round of speculation as the next century comes closer—that can be taken for granted. And several of the issues discussed in these essays will continue to be active into this longer future.

I see no one theme that will, by itself, set the tone for the 1990s. Some developments, however, do seem absolutely certain: (1) a scramble over replacement of retiring faculty members, (2) a great need to replace or renovate buildings and equipment, (3) a great demand by higher education for more resources, with fewer new resources becoming available and with more competition for them, (4) a rising racial/ethnic crisis or crises, (5) continuing pressure on higher education to advance the economy, (6) a leap forward in the internationalization of the curriculum and of academic contacts, and (7) a more pressured situation for mechanisms of governance. Highly likely are (8) a still-increasing interest in the improvement of academic curricula for undergraduates and even (possibly) some improvements, and also (9) a still-rising concern for ethical behavior within higher education—and again (possibly) some improvements. Conceivable, but I think much less likely, are (10) a renewal of *generalized* student activism, à la the 1960s, united against "the establishment," a new "tide of collective action," and (11) a rising sense of dissatisfaction among faculty members. Altogether a real "mince pie."

My own estimate of the greatest challenges for the 1990s are, first, greater devotion to the higher education of now-underserved minorities[1] and, as a result, some greater progress in advancing this aspect of the general welfare; and second, at the faculty level, the search for means to advance diversity while also maintaining excellence.

Let me, as a prelude, make a confession about my past expectations about the future, in the fields of both industrial relations and higher education: My evaluation is that I have had some general sense (as so many others have had also) of the important themes for future development.[2] However, I have had a tendency to be less perceptive about the timing of developments, sometimes expecting them to come faster than they actually have, and in addition a tendency to neglect countervailing forces that sometimes twist and turn the developments into unexpected configurations. Thus, a word of caution!

Chapter 8 takes a general look at the 1990s. Chapter 9 considers the current widespread demand for a restoration of quality to undergraduate education, and chapter 10 the special issue of teaching ethics. Chapter 11 treats the "racial" crisis, and chapter 12 advances a possible solution to the puzzle of selective admissions as related to racial/ethnic status. Chapter 13 examines the competitive situation among institutions of higher education (particularly research universities) within the most competitive system of higher education the world has ever known.

Notes

1. See the discussion in Arthur Levine and Associates, *Shaping Higher Education's Future* (San Francisco: Jossey-Bass, 1989).

2. See, for example, Clark Kerr, *The Future of Industrial Societies: Convergence or Continuing Diversity?* (Cambridge: Harvard University Press, 1983), which set forth a convergence process toward market structures.

CHAPTER 8

Prospects for the 1990s

This essay was prepared as the introductory chapter to a volume on the 1990s. It was intended as an overview of the possibilities for that decade. Consequently, it is centered on alternative scenarios as seen by others as well as my own.

It followed, in historical sequence, a similar chapter that I wrote for a volume on prospects for the 1980s.[1] My theme then, looking ahead, was "a series of short-range problems and not a prospect of a long-term decline" at a time when many others thought they were seeing ahead the greatest and most devastating demographic depression for higher education in American history—at levels of 25 to 40 percent. I thought I saw, on the contrary, no single dominating theme but rather "3000 futures," each separate, that required looking at the disaggregated prospects of single institutions and of small groups of institutions.

This is the way it more or less turned out, except that I expected more of a potential decline in student enrollments by the middle 1990s (in a range centering on 10 percent) than now seems even remotely possible. Howard Bowen came closest, since he foresaw the "possibility" that there might be no decline in enrollments at all. I was, however, more nearly right than almost all others were, but only because I saw a swirling series of forces and counterforces at work and some "wild cards." My confusion about which forces and which wild cards might be the more important saved me from graver errors. My view did lack the clarity of a single overwhelming theme—but so also did that decade in retrospect. I also lack clarity about a single theme for the 1990s, as the essay that follows shows, although I do come very close to choosing one.

Looking backward at the history of higher education in the United States in the twentieth century, I take these five observations to be well founded:

1. Each decade has had its own characteristics.
2. It would not have been possible to predict all of these characteristics with any great accuracy.
3. These characteristics were shaped more by what was happening outside, than inside, the academy; that is, higher education was mostly not in control of its own fate.

TABLE 9

**Percentage Increases in U.S. University and College Enrollments
During the Twentieth Century, by Decade**

Decade	Percentage Increase
1900–1910	49
1910–1920	68
1920–1930	84
1930–1940	36
1940–1950	78
1950–1960	31
1960–1970	120
1970–1980	45
1980–1990	17
1990–2000	13 (projected)

4. Each succeeding generation of leaders within higher education nevertheless has sought to predict and plan for the future, as envisioned.
5. Higher education, regardless of its limited powers of divination, survived
each successive wave of challenges and expanded on a secular basis in size
and functions.

The 1980s almost certainly will not be replicated. To expect that they
will, I believe, is to live with illusions. The 1980s were a nonhistorical decade—nonhistorical in the sense that so little happened that made history. It
was a status quo decade. Enrollments increased moderately. Indeed, as indicated in table 9, the percentage increase in enrollments was the smallest thus
far in the twentieth century. Financing was static. Academic programs were
static. So was much else, as table 10 reveals. 1989 was mostly a replica of
1979. Few important decisions were made, because few important decisions
needed to be made. Decision makers had mostly a free ride. To the extent that
"presidents make a difference,"[2] they make less of a difference in a decade
such as the 1980s. They make more of a difference in times of greater change
and greater conflict, and thus they will be more influential once again in the
1990s. The same can also be said of other decision-making entities, including
boards of trustees, faculty senates, coordinating mechanisms, and governors.
They all had a free ride in the 1980s but will not in the 1990s.

The 1980s were roughly similar, in respect to the easy ride had by governing mechanisms, to two other decades in the twentieth century: 1900 to 1910
and 1920 to 1930. Both of these decades were also periods of "normalcy."

The 1990s will, I believe, fall into a second category of decades with
substantial challenges and changes, along with the following other decades in
the twentieth century:

TABLE 10

811

Changing Dimensions of American Higher Education in the 1980s

Dimension	1980	Change in 1980s		Late 1980s[a]
Enrollments				
Enrollments	12 mil.	+ .8 mil.	=	12.8 mil.
Enrollments in public institutions	9.5 mil.	+ .5 mil.	=	10 mil.
Enrollments in private institutions	2.5 mil.	+ .3 mil.	=	2.8 mil.
Women as percentage of total enrollment	51	+ 2.5	=	53.5
Minorities as percentage of total enrollment	17	+ 1.4	=	18.4
Percentage of blacks aged 20 and 21 enrolled in school or college	23	+ 2.7	=	25.7
Percentage of whites aged 20 and 21 enrolled in school or college	32	+ 1.5	=	33.5
Percentage of freshmen intending to major in business or engineering	36	0	=	36
Degrees				
Number of doctoral degrees conferred	33,000	+ 1,000	=	34,000/yr.
Number of medical doctor degrees conferred	15,000	+ 600	=	15,600/yr.
Faculty				
Size of professoriate	685,000	+ 41,000	=	726,000
Number of faculty covered by collective bargaining agreements	190,000 (1985)	+ 37,000	=	227,000
Institutions				
Number of institutions	3,200	+ 400	=	3,600
Number of public institutions	1,500	+ 100	=	1,600

TABLE 10 (continued)

Changing Dimensions of American Higher Education in the 1980s

Dimension	1980	Change in 1980s		Late 1980s[a]
Institutions				
Number of private institutions	1,700	+300	=	2,000
Enrollment in public institutions as percentage of total	80	0	=	80
Percentage of public enrollment in community colleges and comprehensive colleges and universities	70	0	=	70
Enrollment in community colleges	4 mil.	+.5 mil.	=	4.5 mil.
Enrollment in public comprehensive colleges and universities	2.4 mil.	+.1 mil.	=	2.5 mil.
Federal and state support				
Federal research and development to universities (1980 $)	$4,300 mil.	+1,400 mil.	=	$5,700 mil.
Federal student aid (1980 $)	$10 bil.	+$1 bil.	=	$11 bil.
State expenditures on operations of higher education institutions (1980 $)	$21 bil.	+4.5 bil.	=	$25.5 bil.
Other indicators				
Percentage of students in public institutions in states with coordinating mechanisms and/or consolidated governing boards	94	0	=	94
Number of states with coordinating mechanisms and/or consolidated governing boards	46	0	=	46

TABLE 10 (continued)

Changing Dimensions of American Higher Education in the 1980s

Dimension	1980	Change in 1980s		Late 1980s[a]
Other Indicators				
States with universal access to higher education	50	0	=	50
Estimated accumulated student years in higher education	220 mil.	+ 80 mil.	=	300 mil.

Source: Elaboration of chart I in Clark Kerr, "Prologue," in *The Great Transformation in Higher Education, 1960–1980* (Albany: State University of New York Press, 1991).

[a]Dates vary, 1986 to 1989 as available.

1910–20 World War I: Women's suffrage movement on campus; economic depression and a period of political reaction after World War I

1930–40 The Great Depression: Student movements, including for peace, for trade unions, for socialism, and for communism

1940–50 World War II: GI rush at the end of the war; McCarthy period after the war

1950–60 Korean War: Preparations for the tidal wave of students, including expansion plans for the community colleges and transformational plans for the state teacher's colleges

Two other decades, 1960–70 and 1970–80, were decades of transformational change (see table 11).[3]

For an impressionistic view of the decades, see figure 5, from which we can see that a decade with major changes or conflicts is really the norm.

Some Proposed Scenarios—with Comments

The process of building scenarios is already well under way for the 1990s. At least three cautions are needed as this process moves along: (1) Many scenarios look mostly at a single major aspect of the possible future and not at how several possible aspects may interact and what comparative

TABLE 11

Changing Dimensions of American Higher Education, 1960–1980

Dimension	1960	Change to 1980		1980
Enrollments				
Enrollments	3.5 mil.	+8.5 mil.	=	12 mil.
Enrollments in public institutions	2 mil.	+7.5 mil.	=	9.5 mil.
Enrollments in private institutions	1.5 mil.	+1 mil.	=	2.5 mil.
Women as percentage of total enrollment	37	+14	=	51
Minorities as percentage of total enrollment	10 (1968)	+7	=	17
Percentage of blacks aged 20 and 21 enrolled in school or college	12	+11	=	23
Percentage of whites aged 20 and 21 enrolled in school or college	21	+11	=	32
Percentage of undergraduate enrollment in professional programs	38 (1969)	+20	=	58 (1976)
Degrees				
Number of doctoral degrees conferred	10,000	+23,000	=	33,000/yr.
Number of medical doctor degrees conferred	7,000	+8,000	=	15,000/yr.
Faculty				
Size of professoriate	235,000	+450,000	=	685,000
Number of faculty covered by collective bargaining agreements	0	+190,000	=	190,000 (1985)
Institutions				
Number of institutions	2,000	+1,200	=	3,200

TABLE 11 (continued)

Changing Dimensions of American Higher Education, 1960–1980

Dimension	1960	Change to 1980		1980
Institutions				
Number of public institutions	700	+800	=	1,500
Number of private institutions	1,300	+400	=	1,700
Enrollment in public institutions as percentage of total	60	+20	=	80
Percentage of public enrollment in community colleges and comprehensive colleges and universities	50	+20	=	70
Enrollment in community colleges	400,000	+3,600,000	=	4 mil.
Enrollment in public comprehensive colleges and universities	600,000	+1,800,000	=	2.4 mil.
Federal and state support				
Federal research and development to universities (1980 $)	$1,300 mil.	+3,000 mil.	=	$4,300 mil.
Federal student aid (1980 $)	$300 mil.	+$9.7 bil.	=	$10 bil.
State expenditures on operations of higher education institutions (1980 $)	$4 bil.	+17 bil.	=	$21 bil.
Other indicators				
Percentage of students in public institutions in states with coordinating mechanisms and/or consolidated governing boards	42	+52	=	94

TABLE 11 (continued)

Changing Dimensions of American Higher Education, 1960–1980

Dimension	1960	Change to 1980	1980
Number of states with coordinating mechanisms and/or consolidated governing boards	21	+ 25	= 46
States with universal access to higher education	1	+ 49	= 50
Estimated accumulated student years in higher education	75 mil.	+ 145 mil.	= 220 mil.

Source: Taken from Clark Kerr, "Prologue," in *The Great Transformation in Higher Education, 1960–1980* (Albany: State University of New York Press, 1991).

weight should be given to each. (2) No scenarios can very well be prepared for the unforeseen. And yet the unforeseen has written much of the recent history of higher education. The tidal wave of students of the 1960s was foreseen, but not the nationwide racial revolt, not the Vietnam War, not the consequent student unrest; not the OPEC crises of the 1970s; and not the failure of the demographic depression of the 1980s to put in its widely promised appearance. (3) Some scenarios are "hope for" scenarios and some are "will be" scenarios.

Scenario 1: Driving the Money Changers Out of the Temple

Colleges and universities inherited a protected status as descendants of the churches out of which they originally mostly evolved, and maintained this status as a result of their own high standards of conduct. This status, however, is now under attack as never before, partly because of the national mood of distrust that followed the scandals of Iran-Contra, Ivan Boesky, and the savings and loan industry, and partly because of the conduct of colleges and universities in the areas of athletics, rising tuitions, alleged misconduct in scientific research, and denial of free speech on campus to controversial conservative speakers, among others. Illustrative of the many attacks is Charles Sykes's characterization, in *Profscam*, of higher education as a profession "run amok."[4] The universities "will be saved," it is said, not by themselves, but rather by legislators, governors, parents and students, and perhaps even some trustees, united in revolts against fraudulent practices. The individual

FIGURE 5

**The Decades of the Twentieth Century in Terms of Change and/or Conflict
Involving Higher Education**

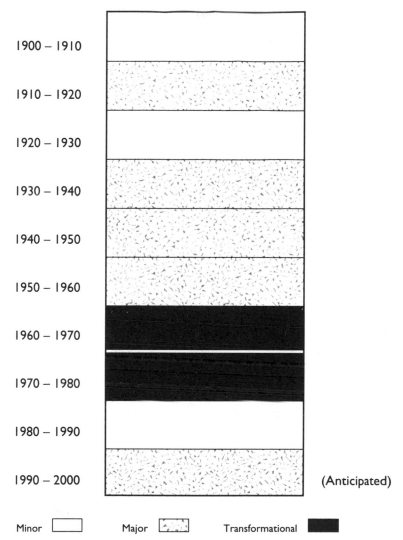

charges in Sykes's indictment are true, but each only to a very small degree. (For a much more balanced discussion, see Bok.)[5]

Depicting these many small degrees as though they were the totality of reality creates an overall totally false impression. Nevertheless, the impression is gaining widespread acceptance. Colleges and universities are falling "from grace." But falling from grace is a long way from a united revolt. The chances of a holy war of purification against the "den of robbers" seem remote to me, however strongly supported by some critics. And it should be noted that colleges and universities, despite a rising tide of complaints, continue to rank among the four American institutions (out of fifteen) in which the American public has the most confidence—along with the military, medicine, and the Supreme Court (Harris Poll, 1990); and they have never (since 1966) ranked below third.

Scenario 2: Restoring the Centrality of Liberal Education

Restoring liberal education to a central position is the theme of Mayhew, Ford, and Hubbard,[6] among others. More attention must be given to the "basics" and to a "core curriculum," as many observers, including me, agree. But the many who agree do not include most of today's students and faculty members. The students, instead, are flocking to the professions (the proportion of enrollments in the arts and sciences has dropped by one-half in recent times), and faculty members, by and large, are pursuing what Bertrand Russell once called the "fiercer specializations," even in the humanities. The rhetoric of tomes on the best-seller lists[7] is not being matched by action at ground level, and I do not think it will be.

Scenario 3: The Coming Racial Crisis in American Higher Education

Racial crisis will be a prominent feature of the 1990s, as seen by, among others, Altbach and Lomotey.[8] Different racial cultures are "living separately, with little knowledge of, or respect for, each other"; and there are "flashpoints of crisis." The trend line of racial incidents on campus is rising. What was once de jure separate but equal has now become de facto more nearly equal but still separate. At the minimum, there will be many demographic realities and opportunities to contend with over the course of the 1990s.[9] The size of the likely college-going population, both young and old, will be slightly smaller, and that population will be composed, in part, of persons who are less adequately prepared academically, less likely to complete their studies to receive a degree, and more likely to require attention to remedial education, financial assistance, and academic, occupational, and personal counseling. However, I do not believe that "these realities point to a period of adversity for colleges and universities as bad as any in the memory of those living today."[10] Those still living today include persons who remember the 1960s and 1970s. One of the greatest opportunities of the decade, nevertheless, will be the consideration given by higher education to the welfare of what have historically been the underserved elements of youth from low-income families and underrepresented minorities.

Scenario 4: The Barricades Rising Once More

"Barricades" yet again is the theme of Whalen and Flacks.[11] Student revolts have been recurrent in the history of American higher education since the early years of Harvard. By the middle 1990s, the last such major revolt will have been thirty years in the past, and the revolt prior to that was yet another thirty years earlier, in the 1930s. The "revolutionary commitment" of the veterans of the 1960s, it is said, still exists (and some are now faculty members), and "the spirit waits for a new opportunity that will permit the tide of collective action once more to rise."[12]

But student bodies (and faculties) are now divided over race, not united by opposition to racial injustice and the Vietnam War; and there are no foreign utopias to inspire and to emulate—not Cuba, not China, not North Vietnam, not Cambodia, not the USSR; and no Che Guevara, no Mao, no Ho Chi Minh, and no Lenin and his vanguard elite. Additionally, small-cohort generations of students historically have been more satisfied and more passive (as the generation of the 1990s may be) than large-cohort generations, which tend to be more dissatisfied and more aggressive (as in the 1960s).[13]

Student revolts have varied so much in goals, from women's suffrage at the time of World War I, to Old Left concepts of socialism and to world peace during the Great Depression, to countercultural aspects of drugs and sexual behavior starting in the earlier 1960s, to racial justice and ending the Vietnam War starting in the middle sixties, and to opposition to apartheid policies in South Africa in the 1980s, that it would be risky to speculate on the goals the next time around or on timing or on chosen means to be employed, ranging from persuasion to violence.

And all the potential parties have changed since the 1960s:

Students are generally more conservative politically than in the 1960s, and higher proportions of them are in engineering, business administration, and other professional schools.

More faculty members may now consider themselves to be on the Left, as products of the 1960s, than at the start of the 1960s, but some of them at least, so it seems, have become more cautious about the use of violence, as they are reported to have been in advising new generations of students on tactics, as in the anti-apartheid efforts of the 1980s, and also more cautious about the use of drugs by their own children. Also, many new faculty members have come out of the "me generation" of the 1970s and 1980s, and the pro-Reagan inclinations, particularly of younger voters, during that period. Additionally, older faculty members in the middle and on the Right, who are also alumni of the 1960s, are more alert to possible excesses by student masses, know one another, and feel more empowered to take leadership from the

Left by experience with the consequences of what happened the last time around and by the collapse of the Left all around the world.

Campus authorities are now more sophisticated in avoiding confrontations, and more likely to quickly turn problems over to the outside police and the law courts, and thus to keep conflicts outside divisive internal decision-making and disciplinary mechanisms—campus autonomy is no longer so highly prized a consideration. And the external police, generally, are more reluctant to use the more harsh means of enforcement.

The public is less easily shocked. And student activism is no longer so new a toy for TV to play with.

If I were to guess at the most likely issue for student activism in the 1990s—if there is one—it would be divisive battles over the racial and gender composition of the new faculties to be employed across the nation, and not a more general tide of "revolutionary commitment" as a reprise of the 1960s. But who knows? Student unrest is the wildest of all wild cards.

Scenario 5: The Increasing Deficits of Ph.D.'s

Demand for new faculty will rise faster than supply as faculty members employed in the 1960s begin to retire and as enrollments start to rise again, and the deficits will be substantial. This scenario is the well-argued expectation of Bowen and Sosa[14] for the arts and sciences. But the much greater crisis at the time of the "tidal wave" of students in the 1960s was handled without substantial damage. Also, as Bowen and Sosa note, there are many processes of adjustment: higher student/faculty ratios, more part-time and short-term appointments, including of those without a doctoral degree, more entrants into Ph.D. programs and shorter periods to completion of the degree,[15] lower quit rates and later retirements by existing faculty, and more recruits from abroad.

Scenario 6: American Professors as an Endangered Species

Bowen and Schuster see a "dangerous but not desperate situation" for professors.[16] Real salary levels have fallen behind national trends, the quality of student preparation has gone down, the faculty has fragmented, bureaucratic controls have increased, more faculty members are part-time and short-term, the quality of physical facilities has deteriorated, fewer of the ablest young people are attracted into the teaching profession, faculty morale has declined, and much else has gone wrong. It might be added that faculty members are more subject to public criticism and to pressures to raise their teaching loads and their general commitment to their campus obligations. But the campus still provides an attractive way of life, most faculty members are satisfied or even very satisfied with their source of employment, and, under the academic labor-market conditions of the 1990s, faculty salaries might rise faster and promotions may come sooner in some fields. It should be a comparatively good decade for the professoriate. The recent survey *The Condition of the Professoriate: Attitudes and Trends, 1989* found that "faculty are increasingly optimistic about their own profession."[17]

Scenario 7: The Accelerating Internationalization of Academic Life

Internationalization will be the great theme for Western Europe in the 1990s, but also a theme for the United States. More students and faculty members will be exchanged among nations. More attention will be paid to world history and to comparative cultures around the globe. Academia is becoming "one world," as banking already has become. The 1990s will be a great decade for global perspectives in education. But a great decade additionally is expected for the biological sciences, and also for the professions of engineering, health care, and teaching.

A Possible Composite Scenario

My own composite scenario, which draws on several of the above, goes as follows.[18]

1. The struggle between equality of opportunity based on merit versus equality of results based on numerical proportionality will intensify. It will be over admissions policies for students at all levels, but particularly also over diversity in the faculty to reflect the new diversity in the student body. Heavy hiring of new faculty members over the next decade and into the early years of the new century creates a context within which struggles over new appointments will go on at the department, school, and college levels as never before in American history. All these little struggles may add up to some big struggles. And both the little and the big struggles will set faculty member versus faculty member and student versus student. Already there have been signs of a backlash among Euro-American and Asian-American students who feel they have been paying and will continue to pay the costs of affirmative action.[19] If I were to try to choose the biggest single issue of the 1990s, it would be in this area of traditional definitions of merit versus equality of results.

2. The push by national economic and political leaders for higher education to make a greater contribution to national industrial competitiveness will also intensify, leading to more and better skills training, and more and better research, particularly in applied areas. This push is particularly strong at the gubernatorial level. I am convinced that both of these expectations

for positive results are higher than the potential ability of higher education to fulfill them within a relatively short time frame, and this can lead to disappointments.

3. The battle for a place in the academic sun will become more fierce, particularly among the research universities. In a period of fifteen years, when there may be a 75 percent turnover or more in the faculty, the chances that some universities will do better than others in the recruitment battles are very high. The historical hierarchy of prestige may be shaken up as seldom, if ever, before—who will win and who will lose?

4. Additional financial resources will be in high demand to advance equality of opportunity, to support increasing competency, to finance competitive recruiting. Also, physical plants and equipment have been aging (nearly one-third of the physical plants in academia were built in the 1960s) and often have been poorly maintained. It has been estimated that plant renovation and replacement will cost $60 billion at current prices against a total investment in physical capital at a replacement cost of $300 billion.[20] Additionally, higher education costs rise faster than for the economy as a whole, since they are not easily offset by increased productivity and historically have not been offset at all. Where will the money come from? In the 1960s, productivity for the economy was rising at a rate of 3 percent a year; now it is at 1 to 1.5 percent. In the 1960s, our nation was the greatest creditor in the history of the world; it is now the greatest debtor. The competition for resources will be ferocious for supporting preschool, primary, and secondary education, for paying off the federal debt, for modernizing the physical infrastructure of the nation, for strengthening the social infrastructure, for supporting economic and political reform around the world, and for much else. And, in the 1960s, the big investment in higher education was clearly supported by vast increases in student enrollments, but this will not be so in the 1990s. And what if there should be a series of recessions as in the 1970s? Regardless of overall consequences for higher education, all institutions will not fare equally. The most vulnerable are likely to be the less selective liberal arts colleges, and these are the institutions that provide much of the diversity within American higher education and that have been so instrumental in introducing previously underrepresented elements of the population—for example, African Americans, Catholics, Protestant Fundamentalists—to advanced education.[21]

5. Higher education will need to put more effort into re-creating its image of integrity and rebuilding the public trust that has eroded over the past thirty years as scandals and complaints have accumulated, and into resisting increased external coordination and control. The two tasks go together, but other forces also encourage outside interference in what have previously been internal affairs. Specifically, there will be greater public demand for more participation by minorities, for attention to conservation of resources within

higher education, for abatement of rising costs of attending college, for attention to teaching, for emphasis on the basics and on liberal education, for contributions to advancement of the economy, for improved teacher education and other assistance to the high schools, and for much else. At present, the burden of these concerns has been carried mostly by the states and, within the states, by the governors. A report for the Education Commission of the States, entitled "Higher Education Agenda,"[22] stated the following:

> We sense a growing frustration—even anger—among many of the nation's governors, state legislators and major corporate leaders that higher education is seemingly disengaged from the battle. Colleges and universities are perceived more often than not as the source of the problems rather than part of the solution. The issues raised are usually specific: lack of involvement in solutions to the problems of urban schools, failure to lead in the reform of teacher education, questions about faculty workload and productivity, and lack of commitment to teaching or the escalating and seemingly uncontrollable cost of a college education. But whatever the issue, the overall sense of many outside colleges and universities is either that dramatic action will be needed to shake higher education from its internal lethargy and focus, or that the system must be bypassed for other institutional forms and alternatives.

6. A place must be reserved for as yet unforeseen events, much as there have been surprises in past decades for higher education.

7. There will be rising pressure, as compared with the 1980s, on decision-making processes within higher education, particularly at the levels of trustees, presidents, and faculty senates. Some existing peril points in the structures of governance may well show up.[23]

It will not be easy to reconcile merit versus proportionality, to meet the demands for improving the economy, to face the competition in the recruitment of a whole new generation of faculty members, to secure additional resources, to restore public trust, to fend off attacks on autonomy, to be ready to handle surprises, and to review and improve decision-making processes.

The 1990s will likely be another decade, among several in this century, to be marked by major changes and conflicts. And higher education once again will survive and grow in size and in complexity of functions.

Notes

This chapter is reprinted from my "Higher Education Cannot Escape History: The 1990s," in *New Directions for Higher Education: An Agenda for the New*

Decade, no. 70, ed. Larry W. Jones and Franz A. Nowotny (San Francisco: Jossey-Bass, 1990), 5–17. Reprinted by permission of Jossey-Bass, Inc.

1. Clark Kerr, "Key Issues for Higher Education in the 1980s" in *New Directions for Higher Education: Preparing for the New Decade,* no. 28, ed. Larry W. Jones and Franz A. Nowotny (San Francisco: Jossey-Bass, 1979), 1–11.

2. National Commission on Strengthening Presidential Leadership (Clark Kerr, Chair), *Presidents Make a Difference* (Washington, D.C.: Association of Governing Boards of Universities & Colleges, 1984).

3. See the discussion in Clark Kerr, *The Great Transformation in Higher Education: 1960–1980* (Albany: State University of New York Press, 1991).

4. Charles J. Sykes, *Profscam: Professors and the Demise of Higher Education* (Washington, D.C.: Regnery Gateway, 1988).

5. Derek Bok, *Universities and the Future of America* (Durham: Duke University Press, 1990). See also his *The President's Report 1988–89* (Cambridge: Harvard University, 1990).

6. Lewis Mayhew, Patrick J. Ford, and Dean I. Hubbard, *The Quest for Quality: The Challenge for Undergraduate Education* (San Francisco: Jossey-Bass, 1990).

7. See, for example, Alan Bloom, *The Closing of the American Mind* (New York: Simon & Schuster, 1987); and E. D. Hirsch, Jr., *Cultural Literacy: What Every American Needs to Know* (New York: Vintage Books, 1988).

8. Philip G. Altbach and Kofi Lomotey, eds., *The Racial Crisis in American Higher Education* (Albany: State University of New York Press, 1991).

9. See the discussion in Arthur Levine and Associates, *Shaping Higher Education's Future* (San Francisco: Jossey-Bass, 1989).

10. Ibid., 170.

11. Jack Whalen and Richard Flacks, *Beyond the Barricades: The Sixties Generation Grows Up* (Philadelphia: Temple University Press, 1989). See also the observation by John H. Schaar, another veteran of the 1960s, that "the present deceptive calm may turn into a whirlwind" (*Legitimacy in the Modern State* [New Brunswick, N.J.: Transaction Books, 1981], 5).

12. Whalen and Flacks, *Beyond the Barricades,* 249, 283. Others have also suggested that this spirit may not have long to wait. See the discussion about the United States in C. Charney, "Rebels with a Cause," *Times Higher Education Supplement,* no. 882 (29 September 1989).

13. Richard A. Easterlin, "What Will 1984 Be Like? Socioeconomic Implications of Recent Twists in Age Structure," *Demography* 15, no. 4 (November 1978): 397–432.

14. William G. Bowen and Julie Ann Sosa, *Prospects for Faculty in the Arts and Sciences* (Princeton: Princeton University Press, 1989).

15. Doctoral awards in the sciences reached an all-time record high in 1988.

16. Howard R. Bowen and Jack H. Schuster, *American Professors: A National Resource Imperiled* (New York: Oxford University Press, 1986).

17. Carnegie Foundation for the Advancement of Teaching, *The Condition of the Professoriate: Attitudes and Trends, 1989* (Princeton: Carnegie Foundation for the Advancement of Teaching), 44.

18. The three top concerns for the immediate future, as expressed by leaders in higher education, are reported to be (1) "public opinion," with increased efforts to offset negative reactions, (2) "state education policy," mostly on financial support, and (3) "demographic trends," including both total enrollments and their compositions (Joel W. Meyerson and Sandra L. Johnson, "Top External Concerns for 1991," *AGB Reports* 32, no. 6 [November-December 1990]: 18–23).

19. See, for example, the discussion by Carl A. Auerbach, "The Silent Opposition of Professors and Graduate Students to Preferential Affirmative Action Programs: 1969 and 1975," *Minnesota Law Review* 72, no. 6 (June 1988): 1233–80. What was once "silent opposition" is now becoming more vocal.

20. Sean C. Rush and Sandra L. Johnson, *The Decaying American Campus: A Ticking Time Bomb* (Boston: Coopers & Lybrand, 1989), a joint report of the Association of Physical Plant Administrators of Universities and Colleges and the National Association of College and University Business Officers, in cooperation with Coopers & Lybrand; and Henry H. Kaiser, *Crumbling Academe: Solving the Capital Renewal and Replacement Dilemma* (Washington, D.C.: Association of Governing Boards of Universities & Colleges, 1984).

21. See the report of the ECS Task Force on State Policy and Independent Higher Education (John Ashcroft and Clark Kerr, CoChairs), *The Preservation of Excellence in American Higher Education: The Essential Role of Private Colleges and Universities* (Denver: Education Commission of the States, 1990).

22. Education Commission of the States, "Higher Education Agenda," planning report presented to the ECS Policy and Priorities Committee, Snow Bird, Utah, 17 November 1989.

23. See the discussion in National Commission on Strengthening Presidential Leadership, *Presidents Make a Difference;* Clark Kerr and Marian L. Gade, *The Many Lives of Academic Presidents: Time, Place, and Character* (Washington, D.C.: Association of Governing Boards of Universities & Colleges, 1986); Clark Kerr and Marian L. Gade, *The Guardians: Boards of Trustees of American Colleges and Universities* (Washington, D.C.: Association of Governing Boards of Universities & Colleges, 1989).

CHAPTER 9

Restoring Quality to Undergraduate Education

I have long been concerned with the declining quality of education for undergraduates in the United States, as shown in my Godkin Lectures[1] at Harvard in 1963: "recent changes in the American university have done them little good" (103). Also, in the Carnegie report Missions of the College Curriculum *(1977)[2] I drafted the section that said that "general education is now a disaster area" (11). Both of these observations came long before the recent spate of reports and best-sellers on the same subject. But I lack faith, after many disappointments, that much will be done. My greatest disappointments have been the failure of efforts to build a better general education program at the University of California at Santa Cruz, a campus that I helped to found, and to spread "global perspectives in education"[3]—a national effort that I once chaired (1976 to 1985).*

This lack of faith in improvements—but not lack of desire for them—is shown in this essay, which was a foreword to a volume produced under the leadership of Lewis Mayhew of Stanford. Mayhew and his associates see "the quest for quality" in undergraduate education as the great theme of the 1990s. I see, and I say this most sadly, more rhetoric than performance. My hopes, however, apparently still spring eternal, for at my suggestion an organization that I cochaired with Robert Atwell, president of the American Council on Education, and under the direction of William Vandament, professor of psychology at California State University, Fullerton, namely, the National Center for the Development of Education, undertook the Registry of Higher Education Reform, *volumes 1 (1989) and 2 (1990).*

My hesitation about results is based on these considerations: First, faculty members, generally, do not show very much interest in "restoring quality to undergraduate education," as compared with pursuit of their academic specialties, and second, students are not urgently demanding it. Mayhew and associates have no greater desire than I do, but they have much higher expectations for effective results in the 1990s. In my judgment, it will be a *theme, but not* the *theme, of the decade ahead.*

This volume, *The Quest for Quality: The Challenge for Undergraduate Education in the 1990s*, is about more than surviving the nineties. It is about the academic quality of undergraduate education in any decade. The same comment can be made equally well about the predecessor volume, *Surviving the Eighties.*[4] It actually was about effective administrative leadership, also in any decade. I view these two volumes as falling not in an historical sequence vertically but in a content sequence horizontally—the one on leadership and the other on an important aspect of what is being led. Both will apply equally well to the first decade of the next century and to succeeding decades, as to the decade just past and the decade just ahead.

The volume on the eighties, in my judgment, was actually not about the eighties as they turned out. It was published in 1979, when the decade of the eighties was expected to involve a struggle to survive, because of the anticipated demographic depression in enrollments (some institutions will find "their very existence jeopardized"). This never happened, although it was the almost universal expectation. There was no test of survival. Yet this in no way takes away from the value of the book, because it is for any time.

So also for the volume on the nineties. It is placed in the context of this single decade, which is a decade of "increased global competitiveness" for the United States, as the authors say. True. But I do not believe that restoring quality to undergraduate education has much to do with global competitiveness in the nineties. It has much more to do with the quality of individual lives and the quality of citizenship over the next half century.

Thus, I recommend this volume, not for its importance particularly for this decade, but as an excellent review of the current status of the nearly eternal problems in the quality of undergraduate education and the means for its improvement in this and any foreseeable decade. I say the same for the prior volume in the area of effective administrative leadership.

Lewis Mayhew (and now, in this volume, with the collaboration of his associates) is as well situated to review undergraduate education as he was to review administrative leadership. I know of no one who has read more widely in the higher education literature than he has or has evaluated more carefully the quality of what he has read. I went back over the footnotes in this volume a second time for this very reason, because I knew that they would provide a well-selected listing of the best of the literature. Lewis Mayhew also has been on, and consulted on, more campuses than anyone else I know. Consequently he has the most comprehensive direct contact with reality to supplement the literature. He is also a devotee of the "golden mean," as I am. Thus, when I have wanted to know what the "current wisdom" about higher education might be, I have asked myself, What is Lew Mayhew thinking and saying? When I have not agreed with him, as I do not to some extent about some of the contents of this volume, I have known that my views are not the "current wisdom."

This leads me to several qualifications.

First, how bad is the situation? The authors point out aspects of undergraduate higher education that have deteriorated:

Less-qualified entering students
More part-time faculty
Spectacular grade inflation
A drastic decline in the attention to liberal education
A parallel decline in the emphasis on basic skills.

I agree. But such evidence as we have—and it is not all that adequate—is that test scores out of college on the average have fallen less than test scores out of high school, which implies, even if it does not prove, that higher education has increased its "value added." I agree that we can and should do better for many reasons, but not so much because we have been doing so much worse. "The War" was *not,* in my opinion, so clearly "lost as far as quality was concerned."

Second, I agree that higher education must improve for the sake of the challenge of global competitiveness facing our nation. Yet we draw more talent from more areas of our society than most of our competitors, and have clearly the best training at the highest levels of intellectual skills and the best basic research in the world. We should improve our performance, but more for the sake of the quality of our total society than for global competitiveness alone.

Third, I agree that the attempted reforms of the 1960s almost universally failed to spread and usually disappeared without a trace. In fact, academic reform in that decade was mostly a colossal failure. The most pervasive "reform" of all was to reduce or eliminate the role of liberal education. (See the Annex to this chapter for a partial listing of reforms initiated in the 1960s— nearly all of which were without positive results. This annex is taken from a presentation I made in Japan in 1976.) But it was important at that time in history to give the spirit of reform a chance, and there was one triumph: greater access. And the "sacrifice of academic quality in the interest of egalitarian gains" was, in my judgment, really not all that great.

Fourth, I agree that "equal share" and "outstanding performance" are, to a degree, in competition with each other, but more in theory than in practice. It is one of the great advantages of the American system of differentiation of functions that it has some institutions concentrating on "equal share" and others on "outstanding performance," and we should keep it that way. Thus I believe that we can do better with both "equal share" and "outstanding performance" at one and the same time—but it will not be easy.

Fifth, I agree with the authors that their rhetoric should worry them that they may be perceived to "worship the status quo." They do show reverence for "parsimony," for "tradition," for "realistic expectations." But if you look at the detail, you will also see the many excellent suggestions they make for improvements in the status quo. They appear to me to be more amelio-rators or even outright reformers than all-out supporters of the status quo ante; to be descendants of the reformers of the 1960s, but descendants who have learned that it is better to be "sound" than just to be experimental. Mayhew and his associates really confront the nineties with a program for substantial improvements. I recommend universal consideration of the many possible reforms that they suggest.

Sixth, I agree that the greater emphasis should now be on "basic skills," "basic courses," "basic student services," and all the other basics; and that this may require some contractionist efforts. But I would not close the door so entirely to expansionist possibilities. The modern American system of higher education was founded on the expansionist philosophy of "any person, any study." Many mistakes have been made in pursuit of this philosophy, but much good service has been provided to American society as well.

All this adds up to saying that Mayhew and his associates express the current wisdom and that the burden of proof lies with those who stand outside it. All policymakers should be fully familiar with their current wisdom—and here it all is in this volume, as it is in the prior volume; a few may also wish carefully to step beyond it—but at their peril. Reading this new volume and rereading the earlier one will make it easier to survive whatever decade the reader may be in, for at least several decades to come.

Notes

This essay was prepared as the Foreword to Lewis B. Mayhew, Patrick J. Ford, and Dean L. Hubbard, *The Quest for Quality: The Challenge for Undergraduate Ed-ucation in the 1990s* (San Francisco: Jossey-Bass, 1990), xi–xiv. Reprinted by per-mission of Jossey-Bass, Inc.

1. Clark Kerr, *The Uses of the University* (Cambridge: Harvard University Press, 1963; rev. 1972, 1982).

2. The Carnegie Foundation for the Advancement of Teaching, *Missions of the College Curriculum* (San Francisco: Jossey-Bass, 1977).

3. See the Study Commission on Global Education, *The United States Prepares for Its Future: Global Perspectives in Education* (New York: Global Perspectives in Education, 1987).

4. Lewis B. Mayhew, *Surviving the Eighties* (San Francisco: Jossey-Bass, 1979).

Annex: Mutations in Undergraduate Education in the United States—Early 1970s

1. Programs for new or nontraditional students

Historically the clientele for American higher education has been young people, aged 17–22. The clientele has included the wealthier segments of society rather than the poorer, more men than women, the intellectually well qualified rather than the intellectually disadvantaged, and a small percentage of the ethnic minority population. Today the traditionally underrepresented groups are enrolling in institutions of higher education in increasing numbers. Colleges are both seeking out such students and creating academic programs for them. In some instances, new institutions have been created for these students.

Examples

A. Programs for adults
   The College of Human Resources in New York, New York, is a two-year private college started in 1964 and is specifically designed to prepare adults for careers in human services.
   The University of Montana, a state university in Missoula, Montana, has developed a network of geographically dispersed local learning centers designed to reach adults in rural Montana.
B. Programs for labor union members
   Empire State College, a public college in Albany, New York, has authorized the creation of a branch campus in New York City designed for people who work with labor union staffs.
C. Programs for women
   Continuing Education for Women at Temple University, an urban university in Philadelphia, Pennsylvania, provides instruction and counseling to women "whose opportunities for skilled employment and self-fulfillment have been limited by the interruption of their education."
D. Programs for Latinos
   DQU in East Los Angeles, California, is a private community college that opened in 1971. It enrolls a student population composed 50 percent of Native Americans and 50 percent of Latinos. DQU offers programs that vary from the traditional to ethnic culture, ranging from two weeks to two years.

E. Programs for convicts

The University of Massachusetts, a public university in Amherst, Massachusetts, offers a program in jails with the purpose of transforming the jail from a custodial to an educational institution.

F. Programs for the poor

The College of the Poor at the State University of New York at Buffalo, an urban public university in Buffalo, New York, is an experimental subunit within the undergraduate college. The College of the Poor offers instruction and counseling designed to increase the chances of the poor students receiving a degree.

Berea College in Berea, Kentucky, is a private liberal arts college that accepts only students unable to afford a college education. All students are required to work ten hours a week at the college.

G. Programs for Native Americans

Navajo Community College in Many Farms, Arizona, is a private community college that offers a very traditional program to Navajos on a Navajo reservation. The college is controlled by the Navajo tribe.

California State University, Humboldt, in Arcata, California, is a public university that offers a program designed to attract and educate Native Americans. This particular program is called the Natural Resources program.

H. Programs for blacks

Nairobi College in East Palo Alto, California, is a private community college that was started in 1969 to educate black leaders in and for black communities.

The University of Ohio in Athens, Ohio, is a public university with the largest enrollment in the United States. Like many other colleges, it offers a program in black studies—the culture and history of black people. These institutions supplement efforts of more than a century to educate blacks in some hundred black colleges, most of which are found in the southeastern region and certain urban centers in the United States.

2. Programs that shorten the length of time required to earn a college degree

The traditional length of time required to earn the undergraduate degree in America has been four years. Innovations for time-shortening include cutting the four-year degree program by one year, attending college prior to secondary school graduation, concurrent enrollment in both secondary school and college, college instruction in the secondary school, and the establishment of a new institution—the early college—that admits students into college at ages fifteen and sixteen, or after two years rather than the traditional four years of secondary school.

Examples

A. Three-year college degrees
   St. Johns University in New York, New York, is a private university that offers a three-year degree by compressing the four-year curriculum. Students enroll for summer study and/or take additional courses during the academic year.
   Francis Marion College in Florence, South Carolina, is a liberal arts school that combines the first two years of college. The academic requirements of the four-year curriculum are reduced by employing intensified interdisciplinary breadth and general education seminars for honors students.
   The State University of New York College at Geneseo in Geneseo, New York, is a public college that permits all students to accelerate their studies by passing general education achievement tests and two-year comprehensive examinations after one year of college attendance.
B. Entrance into college prior to graduating from high school (early admission)
   Shimer College in Mt. Carroll, Illinois, is a private liberal arts college that admits highly qualified students after three years of secondary school. This practice is common for excellent high school students at many universities.
C. Concurrent secondary school and college attendance
   Brandeis University in Waltham, Massachusettss, is a private university that permits secondary school students to enroll in college courses while attending secondary school full-time. The college courses are substituted for secondary school courses in the student's academic program.
D. College instruction in the secondary school
   Appalachian State University in Boone, North Carolina, is a rural public college that trains local secondary school teachers to teach college-level courses in the secondary schools. Some of the secondary school students involved in the program enter college as second-year college students.
E. Early college
   Simon's Rock in Great Barrington, Massachusetts, is a private liberal arts college that admits students after two years of secondary school. After four years of study at Simon's Rock a student can receive a bachelor's degree.

3. Programs that utilize noncourse formats

The traditional medium in which higher education in the United States is dispersed is the course. Alternatives to the course currently in use include competency-based education, which requires mastery by any of several means available to students of a curriculum stated in the form of educational outcomes or objectives; progress by exam, which requires only that students pass a series of comprehensive exams to receive a degree; and contract learning, which involves an agreement between a faculty adviser and a student that requires the academic program to be completed over a span of time.

Examples

A. Competency-based education

Alverno College in Milwaukee, Wisconsin, is a private religious college that states its requirements in terms of outcomes or competencies demanded of graduates. There are eight competencies: (1) effective communication skills, (2) analytical capability, (3) problem-solving abilities, (4) a facility for value judgments and independent decisions, (5) a facility for social interaction, (6) understanding of the relationship between the individual and the environment, (7) awareness and understanding of contemporary work, (8) knowledge of, understanding of, and responsiveness to the arts and knowledge and understanding of the humanities. "Each competence is set forth in a developmental sequence of six stages, and each stage is defined in a manner that facilitates assessment of performance." Competence may be achieved on the basis of past experience, current courses, independent study, work, and so on.

Other campuses with competency programs include Sterling College (a private religious college), Sterling, Kansas; Bowling Green State University, (a program within a public university), Huron, Ohio.

B. Progress by exam

Hampshire College in Amherst, Massachusetts, is a private liberal arts college that requires only that students pass six comprehensive exams to graduate. Four exams are in general education or breadth areas, and two are in the area of major or depth study.

C. Contract learning

New College in Sarasota, Florida, is a liberal arts college that requires that every student meet with his or her adviser to plan a program of study for each term. The agreed-upon program, which is called a "contract," may consist of courses, off-campus study, independent study, or the like. Nine successful contracts are required for graduation.

Other examples: Empire State College (public college), Albany, New York; New College–University of Alabama (subunit in a public university), University, Alabama.

4. Programs that unite education and work

Traditionally the world of higher education has been separate from the world of work. Because attendance at institutions of higher education has demanded a full-time commitment, very few students have been able to go to school and work full-time simultaneously. Furthermore, education designed specifically for work preparation historically has been labeled "anti-intellectual" and has been excluded from universities on these grounds. Today the integration of higher education and work is becoming quite common. Innovative mechanisms for uniting the two include career planning and counseling programs, which seek to aid the student in formulating life and career goals; cooperative education or work-study programs, which mix periods of work and academic study; and vocational-major programs, which permit students to concentrate their study on a vocational or career subject.

Examples

A. Career planning and counseling
   Slippery Rock State College in Slippery Rock, Pennsylvania, is a public college that offers a voluntary four-year, noncredit program called "LEAP," designed to supplement the academic program and compensate for its lack of career orientation. LEAP helps the student in formulating life goals and in gaining experience in potential career areas.
B. Cooperative education or work-study
   Antioch College in Yellow Springs, Ohio, is a private liberal arts college that offers a five-year program of alternate terms of work and study. All Antioch students are required to participate in the program.
   Other examples: La Guardia Community College (public community college), New York, New York; Tunbridge program at Lone Mountain College (students and tutor study field of interest and interview professionals in the field), San Francisco, California
C. Career-major study
   Miami-Dade Community College in Miami, Florida, is a public community college that offers majors in mortuary science, air conditioning, general office careers, landscape development, police science, and teacher assistance.
   The University of Arkansas at Pine Bluff, Arkansas, is a public university that offers major study in automotive technology, brick masonry, and welding technology.
   Today many two-year community colleges and four-year colleges include vocationally and/or occupationally oriented courses.

5. Programs that utilize nontraditional time schedules

Traditionally American higher education has been an enterprise of five, sometimes six days a week, 8 o'clock in the morning through 5 o'clock in the

afternoon. Today higher education programs are utilizing the previously un-
filled time blocks. Night schools are very common. Current innovations in
nontraditional time scheduling include weekend colleges, which offer intensive instruction only on Friday evening, Saturday, and Sunday; and early
morning colleges, which have classes that meet only prior to the start of the
workday.

Examples

A. Weekend college
   C. W. Post College in Greenvale, Long Island, New York (private
   college).
B. Early morning college
   Long Island University in Long Island, New York, a private university, is
   the most extreme example, offering classes that are held on a commuter
   train during the trip between the suburbs and New York City.

6. Programs that are noncampus based

American higher education has historically taken place on the college
campus. Today the walls of the campus are opening to include the greater
society. Innovations in this area include the external degree, which is based
largely upon independent study; credit for life experience, which involves receiving academic credits for prior experiences that are the equivalent of college courses; study by television; employment of a faculty consisting largely
of community professionals who work full-time in nonteaching jobs; the use
of such local or community facilities, such as libraries, storefronts, muse-
ums, railroad stations, neighborhood centers, and fraternal organizations, for
instruction.

Examples

A. External degree
   The Regents External Degree offered by the University of the State of
   New York is based solely upon a series of exams covering the course of
   college studies. Study for the exam is entirely independent and
   undirected.
   Metropolitan State University, a public university in Minneapolis, Minnesota, offers a program that credits past learning, counsels students,
   arranges for independent study, and provides non-campus-based
   instruction.
B. Credit for life experience
   New College at the University of Alabama in University, Alabama,

enrolled a student with over thirty years of professional experience in television, radio, and newspapers. He had written national news documentaries, had edited newspapers, and was the public relations officer for a school board. After the student's experience was evaluated in terms of college study, he was awarded over two years of college credit.

Other notable examples: University Without Walls (consortium of public and private colleges and universities), Yellow Springs, Ohio; Empire State College (public college), Albany, New York.

C. Study by television

Flathead Valley Community College, a public community college in Kalispell, Montana, has the capacity to provide college instruction to 85 percent of the local residents in the Flathead Valley via television.

D. Community faculty

Metropolitan State University, a public university in Minneapolis, Minnesota, has a faculty composed largely of community people who instruct and advise students on a part-time basis.

E. Community facilities

Metropolitan State University in Minneapolis, Minnesota, offers instruction and counseling in storefronts, neighborhood centers, and libraries. Flathead Valley Community College in Kalispell, Montana, offers instructions in a remodeled garage, a railroad station, and fraternal organizations.

7. Programs that emphasize new subjects

Today new institutions with new subject foci are being established.

Examples

A. Environmental studies

University of Wisconsin-Green Bay (public college), Green Bay, Wisconsin.

B. Transcendental meditation

Maharishi International University (private college), Fairfield, Iowa.

C. Human services

College of Human Resources (private college), New York, New York.

8. Programs based in organizations not usually associated with higher education

Today several new educational organizations are springing up. Innovations in this sphere include brokerage organizations, which advise and counsel students, aid students in documenting prior learning, and speak for the student in gaining admission and credit in educational programs both inside and outside the university; and schools organized and operated by industrial organizations.

Examples

A. Brokerage organizations
    The Regional Learning Service of Central New York in Syracuse, New York, offers free counseling and assistance by paraprofessionals to adults interested in educational experiences.
B. Industry-based schools
    Bell and Howell Schools, Chicago, Illinois.

Notes

This Annex is taken from a presentation I made in Japan in 1976. (Clark Kerr, "Current Mutations in Undergraduate Education in the United States," in *Perspectives for the Future System of Higher Education* [Hiroshima: Research Institute for Higher Education, Hiroshima University, in cooperation with the International Council for Educational Development, 1976].)

Comment on the Special Problem of Teaching about Ethics

Related to several issues in chapters 8 and 9, including renewing the sense of integrity and advancing liberal learning, is the teaching of ethics to students. Such teaching once was at the center of the curriculum of departments of philosophy; now it is relegated to the periphery. But the role of ethics can now also be found in many other departments, such as history, political science, the professions, and even the sciences. I would like to see this teaching of ethics spread in the 1990s and beyond, and admire the leadership taken by Sissela and Derek Bok of Harvard.

For the first two centuries and more in the United States, moral philosophy was at the heart of the curriculum, and frequently the president of the college taught the capstone course. This approach was increasingly abandoned, particularly after the War between the States,[1] as training shifted from preparation for the ministry, teaching, law, and medicine to the many and more production-oriented occupations of an industrializing nation, as science and the scientific approach became more dominant within academe, and as America became a more diversified nation in its cultures and in its religious beliefs. Ethics was relegated to a smaller and smaller corner of philosophy as philosophy itself moved toward mathematical logic and the study of the meaning of language. Ethics, it was said, was not subject to proof, and proof is basic to scholarship; and so ethics was increasingly declared to be an off-campus concern in many institutions.

But ethics will not go away.[2] In fact, the teaching of ethics is the great growth industry in many professional schools, including law, business, medicine, and even agriculture and environmental sciences. The professional schools are more in contact with the surrounding society, and the surrounding society is rife with ethical questions. On campus, students have been raising more ethical questions, particularly since the 1960s, and this has forced administrators[3] and boards of trustees to give them greater attention. This has made campus governance more difficult, since issues of ethical conduct are not subject to easy agreement; but as a result, campus governance may be better "morally" in the long run. It can even be said, without too much exaggeration, that higher education is in a crisis of ethics.

I am convinced that consideration of ethics will and should penetrate more into the central curriculum and not just into the professional schools on the periphery. Ethics can be and should be more of a subject for scholarly study. Societies change not just on the basis of changing technology, and people within societies are motivated not only by considerations of material welfare. What people think is right and wrong is also a force at work and can be studied as such. It seems to me that somewhere within the curriculum more attention can be given to ethical issues in a scholarly way, just as we give scholarly attention to critical evaluation in literature and in the arts. At least the following can be done:

Raise the consciousness of students about the general role played by ethics and moral values in the functioning of societies[4] and in their own lives.

Make available scholarly analyses of different ethical systems: how internally coherent they are, what may be held in common and what is different among ethical systems, and how they relate to their societies in their origins.

Present comparative studies of the roles played by ethical systems and moral values in the history of societies,[5] as today in the politics of Iran and the economics of Japan.

Make available examinations of ethical systems within segments of society, such as law, medicine, and business; and even within the conduct of the basic disciplines. Among others, the disciplines of anthropology and psychology have formal codes of ethical conduct.

All this can be done in a scholarly way with emphasis on facts and analysis, and without indoctrination. I agree with Derek Bok that "moral issues can be discussed as rigorously as many questions taken up in more established courses in the curriculum. With the help of carefully selected readings and well-directed discussions, students may learn to sort out all the arguments that bear upon ethical problems and apply them with care to concrete situations." Students can be helped to develop a "capacity to reason carefully about ethical issues."[6] Students are in a developmental stage, and such capacity is part of their development. There is moral knowledge as well as scientific knowledge.

There is one area, however, where I believe that a normative approach is desirable, and that is in the area of academic ethics itself. Academic ethics, most places, is now taught more by example than by direct instruction, and this may possibly be the best way. I recognize the warning of Martin M. Buber, who said, "I have made the fatal mistake of giving instruction in ethics."[7] But I believe it would be helpful to make academic ethics not just implicit through the conduct of professors as role models but also explicit in actual teaching; partly because some professors as role models themselves could benefit from guidelines for their conduct and, also, for the sake of the considered evaluation of faculty members by students. This academic system of ethics can be grounded in the requirements of the effective advancement and transmission of knowledge, and of integrity in relations of faculty to students.[8] The academic world should not practice "value neutrality" about its own ethical values any more than should medicine or law. It should codify and teach its ethics, teach ethics via practice, and should establish an even-handed system of judicial review.

Notes

This paper was presented at the Christian A. Johnson Symposium on Ethics and Values, chaired by Arthur E. Levine, at Bradford College, Bradford, Massachusetts, 11 April 1988.

1. "Dropping all pretensions to wisdom" along the way, according to Edward D. Eddy ("What Happened to Student Values?" *Educational Record* 58, no. 1 [Winter 1977]: 7–17).

2. For good discussions of the teaching of ethics on campus, see Daniel Callahan and Sissela Bok, eds., *The Teaching of Ethics in Higher Education: A Report by the Hastings Center* (Hastings-on-Hudson, N.Y.: Hastings Center, 1980); also Daniel Callahan and Sissela Bok, "The Role of Applied Ethics in Learning," *Change* 11, no. 6 (September 1979): 23–27; also Derek C. Bok, "Can Ethics Be Taught?" *Change* 8, no. 9 (October 1976): 26–30.

3. Much as presidents may seek to avoid the "ethical dimensions" of campus life: "Most presidents would not recognize an ethical dilemma if it hit them broadside. Perhaps their need to survive in order to succeed numbs the troubled conscience" (Harold L. Enarson, "The Ethical Imperative of the College Presidency," *Educational Record* 65 [Spring 1984]).

4. For an excellent discussion of the role of "systems of value-orientation" within the "organization of culture," see Talcott Parsons and Edward A. Shils, eds., *Toward a General Theory of Action* (Cambridge: Harvard University Press, 1962), particularly part 2, chap. 3.

5. A. O. Hirschman, for example, has written most thoughtfully about how the "interests" have been the "tamers of the passions" and have brought about the "downfall' of the "idea of glory," and of the "pitting of passion against passion" in the history of Western civilization (*The Passions and the Interests* [Princeton: Princeton University Press, 1977]). But the "interests" also need to be tamed by some rules governing ethical conduct, and this has been a long and continuing process.

6. Derek Bok, *Beyond the Ivory Tower* (Cambridge: Harvard University Press, 1982), 124. See also Derek Bok, *Universities and the Future of America* (Durham and London: Duke University Press, 1990), esp. chap. 4.

7. Martin Buber, *Between Man and Man* (New York: Macmillan, 1965), 105.

8. See the discussion in chapter 9, "The Academic Ethic and the Professoriate: A 'Distintegrating Profession'?" in Clark Kerr, *Higher Education Cannot Escape History: Issues for the Twenty-first Century* (Albany: State University of New York Press, 1994), chap. 9.

CHAPTER 11

The Racial Crisis in American Higher Education

If I had to pick a single theme most likely to be dominant in the 1990s, it would be "the racial crisis" in its several forms. But that possibility seems less certain to me than it does to some others. This essay was the preface to a book, edited by Philip G. Altbach and Kofi Lomotey, that is the best book I have seen on this subject, even if I am not so convinced as they are of a rapidly ascending crisis. I see, instead, situations getting both worse and better, and as yet unsettled results of the confrontation between the two conflicting series of developments of getting worse and getting better.

"Getting worse" includes the growth of an increasingly hereditary underclass living almost totally outside the mainstream of American life, and seething with hostility; the intensification of the separation of lives by group affiliation on many college campuses; the reduction in the availability of federal student grants in colleges; the realization of the intractability of private conduct among many members of the majority population; the combination of rising expectations and rising disappointments. Ralph Bunche, with whom I served for many years on the board of the Rockefeller Foundation, used to say to us that the worst scenario is to raise expectations and then to disappoint them.

"Getting better" includes the growing numbers of minorities entering the middle class, the success of some minorities in the highly competitive endeavors of competitive sports and competitive entertainment, and the entrance of some minority persons into positions of political leadership.

My first personal contact with the racial problem was when I was an undergraduate student at Swarthmore. I was horrified at what I saw. I had come from a totally white farming community where everybody had all they wanted to eat. Through the American Friends Service Committee, along with another Swarthmore student, I went once a week to an elementary school in the urban slums of North Philadelphia to prepare week-old bread, stale milk, solidified apple butter, and other donations gathered by the Quakers for famished students in the Great Depression. We met no other students from all the other colleges and universities in the Philadelphia area. My second contact came through the athletic trainer at Swarthmore, a lay preacher, who took me along with him to preach the cause of world peace. I met congregations in the black churches. There I felt great faith and hope and tolerance and a spirit of love. I was amazed that a people treated so badly for so long could still be so kind to others. That was sixty years ago, and time is running out.

Along the way, I have been impressed with the importance of looking at all individuals in a multidimensional way—not at any one characteristic alone, particularly if that characteristic is not of the individual's personal choosing. I have also been impressed that society, as far as is possible, should equalize opportunity so that individuals advance and retreat on the basis of their talent and effort and not their inherited status. I have also been impressed with the role of education in affecting how individuals look at other individuals, and in helping to level the playing fields of economic, political, and cultural life.

The Racial Crisis in American Higher Education reads to me, in its totality, like the famous passage from the Book of Daniel. In case you have forgotten: "Thou art weighed in the balances, and art found wanting." However, this volume does not go so far as to say, as does the Book of Daniel, "Thy kingdom [is] finished." The central message is that higher education, in its policies toward minorities and its treatment of them, has been found wanting, and that there have been, and will be, even more serious consequences.

The injunction is that the greatest single imperative before American higher education currently is to improve its performance in this crucial area. I agree that this is one of the great imperatives now before higher education but would suggest that there are others, including, but not limited to, (1) responding to the demands of our society for higher education to make greater contributions to our national economic competitiveness, and (2) renewing our faculties and facilities in a short period of time to replace those recruited and built in the 1960s and early 1970s. The first of these two poses a great contradiction—it places a very heavy emphasis on merit alone, while the treatment of minorities includes an emphasis on compensatory opportunities. The second, however, is a complementary force, since it will open up many new faculty positions for possible appointments of minorities.

I have spoken of this volume "in its totality" and will also comment further upon it "in its totality," but this, I fully realize, is somewhat misleading—for there are altogether fifteen essays involving nineteen authors. Each essay has, of course, its own themes and emphases. However, they do add up to one overall and consistent impression that all is not well! This theme is quickly stated by the two editors, Philip G. Altbach and Kofi Lomotey—both at the State University of New York at Buffalo, in the introduction and the first chapter. Lomotey writes of different racial cultures "living separately, with little knowledge, or respect for, each other"; and Altbach of how racial issues in American higher education have been and are at "flashpoints of crisis."

A few of the major themes that run through these essays are these:

Racism is a problem of all of American society, not of higher education alone; yet higher education is now on the front lines of the conflicts, as were once the buses, the lunch counters, the city streets, the factory employment offices. Too much of a burden, however, is now being placed on higher education to find solutions that it, by itself, cannot possibly find.

The numbers are better than they once were, as in the early 1960s, but still not adequate either in admissions or in completion rates, except for Asian Americans. The special case of Asian Americans splits the minorities among themselves. Their interests and their favored policies not only are not the same but actually opposed to those of other minorities.

Nothing works as well as it should—not student aid, not affirmative action. The results, consequently, are not commensurate with the efforts. And additionally, numbers alone are not enough of a test of performance.

While the numbers are better, the relations are worse. Some minorities get more, but they then come to expect more—their own residence halls, their own courses, and their own academic enclaves. Simultaneously, what is called in one essay the "arrogant majority" is becoming more resentful of what it views as special privileges given to minorities. "Hostile stereotypes" of each other are intensifying. The number of racial incidents on campuses is increasing. Both the lash and the backlash are stronger.

The most preferred new solution is required courses to improve racial understanding. Yet there can always be problems with compulsory courses in a student body intent on individual choices, and the courses may turn out to be counterproductive.

The central persons in all of these growing conflicts are the college and university presidents, and next the faculties at large; and neither is as yet taking the intensifying problems with sufficient "seriousness."

Overall, we have been moving from "separate but equal" (de jure) to "equal but separate" (de facto); and separation and some antagonism are still harsh facts of American life, including on campus. There is a new situation in the United States: the old ethnic minorities wanted to be included in the mainstream of national life, but some members of the new racial minorities reject the mainstream culture.

I agree with all of the above. And this volume pulls it together as I have never seen it done before. The episodes I have known about separately are joined together into a more complete and even overwhelming general view. I have taken the situation very seriously for many years but even more so now that I have read these essays. Higher education may well be even closer than I had previously believed to "flashpoints" that might ignite a larger flame.

However, there are some other and more favorable developments that this volume does not emphasize:

More and more blacks and Hispanics are entering middle-class status—and some of the problems have been of class as well as of race.

Education, including higher education, has been the chief line of advancement for disadvantaged minorities, and they know this.

The academic world is now more open to the advancement of disadvantaged minorities, because of both the slackening of enrollment pressures in the early and mid nineties, and the large numbers of replacements of retiring faculty members now in prospect.

Public opinion polls show that there exists, among the general public, both majority and minority, a rising mutual understanding and tolerance.

In handling conflicts, we seem to have learned from the 1960s. The activists and the police both seem to have concluded (so far at least) that the introduction of violence on campus can be counterproductive. Witness the contrast between the generally peaceful handling of antiapartheid demonstrations in the 1980s as compared with many violent episodes in the 1960s when both sides were more intent on violent confrontation.

These considerations, if taken into account, lead to a less alarming view of the developing situation, but still to grave concern; and I recognize that the writers of these essays are generally closer to the front lines than I now am, and I did leave this book with even more concern than when I started to read its pages.

Having said this, let me quickly add that some very fundamental philosophical issues are involved here:

How much to emphasize merit versus how much to emphasize compensatory opportunities? And how much to emphasize opportunity as against how much to emphasize proportionality of results?

How much to emphasize free speech and free actions associated with free speech versus how much to emphasize and protect the sensitivities of individuals?

These are inherently more difficult issues than ending discriminatory racial laws, and it will take much more time to work out solutions that may obtain general consent. And experience to date shows how much easier it is to change public policies than to change private behavior.

These essays place a great deal of responsibility on the leadership of the college and university president in developing policies and in handling crisis situations. The authors do not demonstrate, however, it seems to me, sufficient understanding of the difficult position of the president. The president can influence many things but can control almost nothing: not the faculty, not the activist students, not the reacting students (including in the fraternities), not the external police, not the board of trustees, not the media, not those vagaries of fate that have so often intervened in crisis situations. In a crisis, so much can go wrong, and yet everything must go right to get a universally satisfactory result, and it seldom does. I can see a casualty rate ahead higher among presidents than in any other element involved. One way to read the four excellent case studies is from the point of view of the president involved, as I did with great attention to the detail.

The 1990s will not be the 1960s nor the 1980s nor any past decade. A new world is being born. One set of statistics—minorities as a percent of total U.S. population:

1950: 12 percent
1980: 15 percent
1990: 20 percent
2000: 30 percent (census estimate)
2050: 45 percent (census estimate)

The frequently unhappy college students in 1990 (the minorities) may become a frequently unhappy much greater percentage within the foreseeable future.

The history of the decades ahead will be written by the actions of many people, by the inputs of many forces—both unfavorable and favorable to constructive solutions, and by the vagaries of fate. *The Racial Crisis in American Higher Education* alerts us, once again, to how much is at stake for the nation and for higher education; and to how complex are the factors at work, and the attitudes, and the philosophical issues; and to how elusive are the solutions. May it be true, as William James once said, that ''great emergencies and crises show us how much greater our vital resources are than we had supposed.''

Notes

This essay was written as the Preface to *The Racial Crisis in American Higher Education*, ed. Philip G. Altbach and Kofi Lomotey (Albany: State University of New York Press, 1991). Reprinted by permission of the State University of New York Press.

Solving the Selective Admissions Dilemma:
A Two-Stage Model for Higher Education

The following article accompanied the intense public arguments over the famous Bakke case, and followed many discussions within the Carnegie Council on Policy Studies in Higher Education that led to the report Selective Admissions in Higher Education.[1] *That report concerned student admissions and suggested ways in which "racial (and ethnic) experience" can most appropriately be taken into account in the academic world. A related problem is the extent to which racial and ethnic experiences can most reasonably be taken into account in faculty appointments and promotions, and another Carnegie report,* Making Affirmative Action Work in Higher Education,[2] *discussed the faculty area. We there suggested, as we had in an earlier Carnegie report,[3] that "the most qualified candidates be chosen with some reference, where appropriate to the position to be filled, for example, as, in areas where a personal history can heighten sensitivities that enhance understanding; to the potential contributions of women and minorities as inspiring 'models' and as helpful 'mentors' "; in other words, a policy of looking at the total prospective contributions of the individual candidate and not just at purely "academic" qualifications as historically defined. Some faculty members as models and mentors, of course, may be more inspiring or helpful than others, and thus individual performances must be taken into account in promotions just as in "academic" achievements.*

In relation to both students and faculty members, the emphasis is to be placed on individual minority racial (and/or ethnic) experiences and not on race (or ethnic status) alone. Racial/ethnic experience usually is a handicap to students but might even be an asset to some faculty members (as we recommended). However, students of minority racial/ethnic background are not always disadvantaged, or faculty members advantaged. Thus we emphasized individual experiences: for students, for example, growing up in a home where English is not the language of common usage or going to a school with low average performance in completion rates and/or in student test scores, or coming from a family with low levels of parental education. And there are, of course, students

with disadvantaging experiences that are not necessarily racial or ethnic in their sources. With the current emphasis on racial/ethnic status,
there is a tendency to neglect income-class impacts: Yet "a student from
a high family income background has eight to thirteen times greater
chance of having a baccaulaureate degree by age 24 than does a student from a low family income,"[4] and low family income is not solely
related to racial/ethnic status.

What is most central is the ability to overcome handicaps, however im-
posed; to show talent and effort within the context of surrounding
circumstances; to demonstrate merit in rising above disadvantages.
Disadvantaged individuals, however, are currently found disproportionately among minority racial and ethnic groups.

A corollary to admission, in part on the basis of disadvantaging experiences, is that students so admitted should be given special assistance
by the college or university so that their disadvantages will be remedied
as quickly and completely as possible—the assistance should be commensurate with the disadvantages. Many institutions consider that their
responsibilities are discharged by the act of admission. Better tests are
the graduation rates and academic performances of students so admitted. Few colleges and universities utilize these better tests of the fulfillment of their responsibilities. And some colleges and universities
make a "record" by taking in mostly advantaged individuals from minority racial and ethnic groups. The real record of value is advantaging
the truly disadvantaged.

The general theme of this proposal for public policy is aggressive affirmative action to remedy disadvantages beyond their control experienced by individuals of all racial, ethnic, and gender backgrounds,
while fully recognizing that such disadvantages are more highly concentrated in some segments of the population than others. This emphasis on individuals is both more acceptable to the American population
at large[5] and more directed toward equality of opportunity across the
board now that increasing proportions of disadvantaged minorities
have entered middle-class status, and now that the problems are more
concentrated in those elements of minority groups that have not entered
middle-class status. Also, it is a burden on all minority students to imply that they were not fully qualified on academic grounds alone.

Viewed broadly and historically, we are now in the second stage of distributing opportunity in the United States by means of higher education.
(1) In the first stage, greater opportunities were given particularly to
the already more advantaged Euro-Americans, with special attention to
those thought to evidence the greater merit. (2) In the current stage, we

are now extending opportunities in the same manner to African Americans, Hispanic Americans, Asian Americans, Native Americans. (3) I believe that the third stage, already emerging, will be and should be to concentrate more on the less advantaged in each of these groupings in an effort to find and develop talent. Educational opportunities will then be distributed more in proportion to individual talent throughout the population and less in proportion to inherited advantages as among and within ethnic groupings. This third stage will better serve social justice, political tranquility, and economic effectiveness.

One major qualification about the viewpoints that follow: We greatly underestimated the time it would take "to overcome the consequences of past discrimination." We said "less than one generation"—the year 2000.

The "we" in the discussion that follows refers to the Carnegie Council, which deliberated at length on this issue. I had been asked to explain the views of the council, which I chaired.

Long before Allan Bakke filed his well-known lawsuit against the University of California, academicians and college administrators throughout the United States were acutely aware of the serious issue of "reverse discrimination" in college admissions.

Bakke charges that his right to equal protection under the law was violated when he was refused admission to the medical school of the University of California at Davis, while minority students with lesser academic credentials were admitted under a special admissions system. The California Supreme Court ruled in Bakke's favor, and the regents of the University of California have appealed that ruling to the United States Supreme Court. A decision is expected this spring [1979].

In addition to the constitutional questions that Bakke has raised—the right to equal opportunity versus the right to equal protection under the law—many individuals in the academic world see the Bakke case as a challenge to the right of a university to pursue policies of affirmative action, and specifically to give consideration to a person's race in making admissions decisions.

The importance of this case to higher education—and to American society—is enormous. The admissions policies of the so-called gatekeeper schools, such as law, medicine, and dentistry, exert a powerful and often controlling influence on who may practice certain critical professions in this country, and also control access to positions of influence and high economic and social reward. Obviously, the broad interest of the whole society is powerfully affected.

The Bakke case has focused national attention on a controversy that has been the center of much attention in legal and academic circles for years. Just what is good academic and public policy in admissions? How much autonomy should a school have in deciding who is admitted to its programs? When does the federal government have the right to step in, and to what degree should that intervention be allowed?

With the assistance of the Educational Testing Service, the Carnegie Council on Policy Studies in Higher Education, an activity of The Carnegie Foundation for the Advancement of Teaching, conducted a six-month study of the complex issue of selective admissions. In the report of our findings, *Selective Admissions in Higher Education,* we have outlined broad boundaries within which we believe lie many acceptable courses of action for institutions of higher education.

Let me state at the outset our position on considering race in admissions. The Carnegie Council believes that the racial experience of an academically admissible applicant—one who meets the impartial academic standards required for successful completion of college or university work—is among the criteria relevant to admissions decisions. Race not only may but should be considered in the final selection where, in the case of an individual, his or her racial identity reflects prior adverse circumstances or a promise to contribute to the educational experience of other students or to the diversity of services to be provided to society.

When groups that have suffered discrimination are heavily underrepresented in the privileged roles resulting from selectivity in higher education, there are grounds for making special efforts to find, prepare, and admit qualified individuals from those groups. In any race, if each runner begins at a different starting line, how can choosing the winner by judging who finishes first be a fair measure of accomplishment? So it is with the contest for admission to the limited number of places in selective schools. Is it within the American spirit to decide who should be awarded the "prize" of a place in graduate school by measuring test scores and grades alone? We think not. Instead, we feel that judging how far a person has come to reach the finish line—what obstacles he or she has overcome in the process—deserves consideration, along with test scores and grades in determining who gains admittance to graduate schools.

The council also believes that race and other minority status can be considered in admissions decisions without lowering academic standards or causing unfair disadvantage to other students. To help colleges and universities with the difficult task of establishing such admissions policies, we are proposing a two-stage admissions procedure.

Today, selective graduate and professional schools not only have many more applicants than they can admit, but they have many more *qualified* applicants than they can enroll. Thus, the first step an institution should take in the admissions process is to eliminate from consideration those applicants who do not meet the minimal standard of admissibility. This standard should be set at the lowest level at which there is a reasonable chance of success in completing the institution's course work without reduction in academic or professional standards. Race, sex, or other minority status is clearly not a consideration here. One source of help in determining this level is to look at the level of, say, ten years ago, when competition for admissions was less intense but competent graduates and practitioners were being trained. Using this standard to determine a pool of qualified applicants will almost certainly result in a larger pool than that now receiving individual consideration by many schools.

In step two of the admissions process—selection—racial experience should be considered, along with traditional criteria for selecting students: scholastic test scores; grades; special interests or abilities; special skills, such as athletic or musical talent; special identities, such as religious or alumni affiliation; ability to contribute to a campus tradition; ability to contribute to the diversity of the student community; and so on.

We emphasize considering racial experience, not race per se, and experience in a non-English-language home, not "heritage" or "surname" per se. We also emphasize considering racial experience *in individual cases.* Most persons with a minority racial background or who are raised in a non-English-language home will have one or more of the characteristics that we believe warrant special consideration: prior adverse social discrimination, prior educational disadvantage, experience with a minority culture, or interest in special services to society. However, not all members of minority groups have these characteristics; in fact, individuals who are not members of minority groups often can possess one or more of them. Thus, it is essential to judge each individual applicant on his or her own merits, and to process all applicants through the same set of admissions procedures.

Though the council strongly supports affirmative action programs, we draw a clear and careful distinction between the use of "quotas" and "goals" in selective admissions. We believe that numerical quotas, which we define as fixed, permanent sets of numbers, should not be used in admissions policies. Instead, we favor setting and striving for goals that can change over time as conditions change, or that can be exceeded or remain unmet in a given year as conditions warrant.

Potential talent must be able to rise from all sources in society, but in the form of qualified individuals, not in the form of rigid numbers assigned in advance. It is individual talent that should be recognized and given a chance to advance in accordance with the effort that accompanies it. This is the way to encourage motivation, to draw forth energies, to inspire the desire to compete and excel. Members of all groups must know that advancement is possible but not guaranteed.

In admissions policies, it is important that flexibility be maintained, and that schools have maximum latitude in exercising judgments about the admission of individual students. Extensive involvement of faculty members in reviewing and classifying individual applications is essential.

The judgment of courts, or legislatures, or government officials should not replace professional judgment except when clearly required by the public interest. Public and academic policy would be at cross-purposes if, for example, public policy were to lead to a reduction of academic standards, or if academic policy obstructed affirmative action or was not otherwise fair and reasonable. But they need not diverge. The challenges are to apply public policy without undue interference with academic judgments and concerns, and for institutions to satisfy public policy without loss of academic standards. Meeting these challenges calls for the most careful consideration, and full attention to complexities and differences and even fine distinctions. There are no universal, mechanical solutions.

In essence, we recommend a fairer chance for all young Americans, offsetting to the extent reasonably possible the consequences of prior educational disadvantage and social discrimination, with preferment based on individual characteristics, effort, performance, and promise.

What we have tried to find is a golden mean that draws on several American ideals so that no one basic ideal in its entirety is rejected in the name of another. We have not discovered a panacea, nor a uniform approach to admissions that we would recommend to every school. Instead, we have tried to lay a foundation upon which individual schools may build their own structures for making admissions decisions. We believe our recommendations meet the tests of constitutionality, respect individual rights, promote the educational ends of institutions, and fully recognize the pressing societal obligations to put an end to racial discrimination.

We hope that, in the future, race and other minority status will be much less a distinguishing feature of American society as we overcome the consequences of past discrimination in education and elsewhere. We also hope that the current period of transition will not last longer than the end of the twentieth century—less than one generation.

Changes will be taking place in the schools and colleges and society in the meantime, and policies should be adjusted as these changes occur. Significant progress has already been made within higher education, but there is still a substantial way to go. Race or background in a non-English-language home will, over time, become less important considerations. In the meantime, in making selective admissions to institutions of higher education, consideration of special characteristics that often derive from such backgrounds is a major means for American society in its efforts to become more just and more integrated.

Notes

This chapter was first published as "Solving the Selective Admissions Dilemma: A Two-Stage Model for Higher Education," *National Forum, Phi Kappa Phi Journal* 58, no. 1 (Winter 1978): 4–6. Reprinted by permission of *National Forum*.

1. Carnegie Council on Policy Studies in Higher Education, *Selective Admissions in Higher Education* (San Francisco: Jossey-Bass, 1977).

2. Carnegie Council on Policy Studies in Higher Education, *Making Affirmative Action Work in Higher Education* (San Francisco: Jossey-Bass, 1975).

3. *Priorities for Action: Final Report of the Carnegie Commission on Higher Education* (New York: McGraw-Hill, 1973).

4. *High School Graduates and College Prospects of Young Adults by Family Income Backgrounds, 1920 to 1980* (Iowa City: American College Testing Service, 1990).

5. For a discussion of how majorities of both blacks and whites consistently favor compensatory action (as in Head Start) and oppose preferential treatment (as in quotas), see Seymour Martin Lipset, *Two Americas* (Fairfax, Va.: Institute of Public Policy, George Mason University, 1991).

CHAPTER 13

The New Race to Be Harvard
or Berkeley or Stanford

This chapter is based on a presentation I made on 17 January, 1989 at one of the aspiring research universities—Arizona State in Tempe. The impression that I got from the audience of deans, departmental chairs, senate leaders, and university administrators was that their university was destined to move up because of its advantaged location—and there are good reasons for these expectations. I got less of an impression that each person was thinking about what his or her area of responsibility could do to accelerate this inevitable movement. I have had these same impressions elsewhere, and taken together they puzzle me. Some persons seem to be less analytical than they might be about the advantages (and disadvantages) of their locations. Others appear to think that their unit is doing the best it can, and that it is other units of the institution that need to try harder. Some individuals aggressively do not want to be pushed to ''move up''—one department chairman at Berkeley once told me: ''Every department has the fundamental right not to be any better than it wants to be.'' I think I have seen more in the way of thoughtless aspirations for the institution than of careful analysis, more confident self-satisfaction than situations always warranted, and also more resistance to improvement than might be wished. Consequently, I believe that there will be more self-inflicted disappointments than surprising successes as aspirations outrun attainments.

I would add to the discussion below an additional comment that, in the ''new race,'' the private universities may generally be in an advantaged position versus the public. The private institutions, it is true, are facing problems with the receipt of money for overhead on federal research contracts, but the publics in most states have the more fundamental difficulties of depleted state budgets. The privates have this great advantage: Average family real income after taxes for the top 1 percent income group has gone up 136 percent from 1977 to 1992, while income for the other 99 percent has remained roughly constant; and this same 1 percent has had its tax bill reduced by $84 billion[1] per year in real dollars. This 1 percent has seemed to be willing to share its enormous gain by way of gifts to private colleges and universities, and this helps

to explain the great success of many of their endowment campaigns.
The public institutions rely much more on taxes paid by the other
99 percent.

All twenty-four hundred "nonspecialized" institutions of higher education in the United States aspire to higher things. These aspirations are particularly intense among the approximately two hundred research and other doctorate-granting universities with 30 percent of all enrollments.[2] These aspirations grow not only out of internal desires but also out of the expectations of members of their communities—their alumni, their states, their related industries and professions. The next two decades are likely to see an enhancement of such aspirations for at least two reasons: (1) The times will present unusual opportunities to move up or down in academic ratings, and (2) the pressures for economic advancement of regions via their research universities will be greater than ever.

I have chosen the title I have given this essay because I have heard so many inauguration addresses and read of others promising that such and such an institution was going to become the Harvard of Southeast state X, or the Berkeley of Southwest state Y, or the Stanford of Central state Z.

Four things, at least, can be said about the race to be better among research and doctorate-granting universities:

- It is natural and eternal in the American context, but increasing in intensity.
- Few institutions, however, improve their positions very dramatically in the course of this race, or decline dramatically, over short periods of time.
- Improvements are more likely to take place at some times than at others.
- Such improvements as do take place depend both on what institutions do and on where they are.

The Pace of Changes

The pace of changes has been slow—with exceptions. The first attempt at reputational rankings was in 1906, and it listed fifteen institutions. Table 12 lists the universities in the 1906 ranking matched against the order of the top fifteen in 1982. (See table 13 for a full listing of the major rankings from 1906 to 1982.)

These listings demonstrate that a reputation once attained usually keeps on drawing faculty members and resources that sustain the reputation. A reputation, once established, is an institution's single greatest asset. These listings also imply that, whatever may be the sources of the reputation to begin with, they will mostly continue to support the reputation.

TABLE 12

The Stability of Reputational Rankings, 1906 and 1982

1906	1982
1. Harvard	California (Berkeley)
2. Columbia	Stanford
3. Chicago	Harvard
	Yale
4. Cornell	
5. Johns Hopkins	MIT
6. California (Berkeley)	Princeton
7. Yale	Chicago
8. Michigan	UCLA
	Michigan
	Wisconsin (Madison)
9. MIT	
10. Wisconsin (Madison)	
11. Pennsylvania	Cornell
	Columbia
12. Stanford	
13. Princeton	Illinois (Urbana)
14. Minnesota	Pennsylvania
15. Ohio State	Cal Tech

Sources: *For 1906:* James McKeen Cattell, *A Statistical Study of American Men of Science*, reprinted from *Science*, ser. 2, vol. 24 (1906): 739. Peers selected the top one thousand men of science by fields; the table gives their distribution according to position/institution at the time of the survey. Government bureaus are omitted.

For 1982. David S. Webster, "America's Highest Ranked Graduate Schools, 1925–1982," *Change* 15, no. 4 (May-June 1983): 18. Based on the number of programs in each field (physical sciences and mathematics, humanities, english, biology, and social sciences) with standard scores of 60 or higher in reputation for "faculty quality" in Lyle V. Jones, Gardner Lindzey, and Porter E. Coggeshall (eds.), *An Assessment of Research-Doctorate Programs in the United States* (Washington, D.C.: National Academy Press, 1982).

Over the nearly eighty years from 1906 to 1982, only three institutions (Johns Hopkins, Ohio State, and Minnesota)—dropped out from those ranked as the top fifteen—but, in each case, not by very much and only three (Illinois, UCLA, and Cal Tech) were added. Only two institutions (Columbia and Cornell) fell five places or more, and only three (Berkeley, Princeton, and Stanford) rose five places or more. And none of these changes occurred rapidly. Let me note quickly, however, that reputational ranking is not a science—it relies on personal judgments, which can be both faulty and prejudiced.

TABLE 13

Seven Major Reputational Rankings of Graduate Schools, 1906–1982[a]

Year of Publication (Year of Basic Data)	1906 (1903)	1925 (1924)	1934 (1934)	1959 (1957)	1966 (1964)	1970 (1969)	1982 (1980)
Harvard	1	2	1[b]	1	2	2	3[b]
Columbia	2	3	3	3	7	12	11[b]
Chicago	3	1	5	6	9	7	7
Cornell	4	10	6	9	11	11	11[b]
Johns Hopkins	5	7	9	16	13	19	30[b]
California (Berkeley)	6	9	1[b]	2	1	1	1
Yale	7	4	7	4	6	5	3[b]
Michigan	8	8	8	5	4	4	8[b]
MIT	9	19	16		21	15	5
Wisconsin (Madison)	10	5	4	8	3	6	8[b]
Pennsylvania	11	12	14[b]	11	15	14	14
Stanford	12	14	13	13	5	3	2
Princeton	13	6	11[b]	7	10	8	6
Minnesota	14[b]	13	10	12	12	16	16[b]
Ohio State	14[b]	15	14[b]	18	22		
Illinois (Urbana)		11	11[b]	10	8	9	13
Iowa		16	17[b]				
Bryn Mawr		17	24[b]				
Cal Tech		18	17		18	20	15
Northwestern		20	21	17	17		18
Missouri		21	19[b]				
Indiana (Bloomington)		24		15	19	18	21[b]
New York University			22	19	23		21[b]

Institution					
UCLA		14	14	10	8[b]
Washington		20	16	13	19
Texas (Austin)	23		20	17	16[b]
North Carolina (Chapel Hill)	24[b]			24[b]	20
Purdue			24	21	25[b]
Brown			25	23	25[b]
Duke				22	25[b]
California (San Diego)					21[b]
Rockefeller					21[b]

Sources: James McKeen Cattell, *A Statistical Study of American Men of Science*, reprinted from *Science*, ser. 2, vol. 24 (1906): ; and David S. Webster, "America's Highest Ranked Graduate Schools, 1925–1982," *Change* 15, no. 4 (May-June 1983): 14–24.

[a]Institutions that have ranked at least twice among the top 25, or only once, but that once was in 1982.
[b]Indicates a tie for the rank.

The exceptions to slow change are few. There have been instant successes—Johns Hopkins in the 1870s, Stanford and Chicago in the 1890s, and the University of California–San Diego in the 1960s and 1970s[3]—and only one rapid decline, when Stanford and Chicago decimated the faculty of the newly founded Clark University in the 1890s.

The Timing of Changes

The timing of reputational changes has been significantly affected by periods of great transformations—first after the War between the States until 1900 and then from 1960 to 1980—the former when the great research universities were first being created, the latter when great expansions of research activity occurred primarily under federal financing, especially after Sputnik. The great advances in the former period were Johns Hopkins, Stanford, and Chicago, and in the latter period in California: at Berkeley, Stanford, Cal Tech, UCLA, and UC–San Diego.

The period 1990 to 2010 may be another period of change in rankings. At least three-fourths of faculties will turn over, and there will be some net additions as enrollments rise over these two decades.[4] Some institutions will do better, and some will do worse, in the quality of their recruitments. I expect some possible advances, this time around, particularly in the South and Southwest.

The Where of Changes

Outstanding research universities are more likely to develop in some places than in others:

- In leading centers of the historic professions, particularly law, medicine, and banking, as once, and still, in Boston, New York, and Philadelphia; and later, and still, Chicago; and still later, San Francisco and Los Angeles.
- In growing centers of progressive economic activity, such as the Midwest once was with its supremacy of agriculture and heavy industry—thus the Big Ten and Chicago; and more recently California, Arizona, and some parts of the South, and the "silicon" areas—including Boston, mid New Jersey, Denver, Austin, the Research Triangle, the Bay Area, and Portland (Oregon); and in centers of concentrated governmental activity—most specifically, the Washington, D.C. area; and in renovating centers, such as Pittsburgh.

- In larger cities more than in small towns, and particularly now in the larger cities for the sake of career-development opportunities for spouses of faculty members, and particularly now also in the larger cities that are hubs for jet airlines so that faculty members can come and go—the recently emergent hubs, for example, in Atlanta, Dallas–Fort Worth, and Pittsburgh.
- In rich communities with a cultured establishment, such as Boston and Philadelphia and New York, historically, and later in Chicago and San Francisco—for the sake of private universities; and in large and rich states, such as Michigan and California—for the sake of public universities. Contrast these areas with some in the deep South with lesser intellectual traditions and more poverty.
- In areas with effective and committed political leadership, as with Governor Rockefeller in New York, Governor "Pat" Brown in California, Governor Kean in New Jersey, and Congressman Magnuson in Washington; and areas with aggressive industrial leadership, such as Pittsburgh and Minneapolis now. At the other end of the spectrum are states with historically highly politicized approaches detrimental to their universities, such as Texas, Colorado, and Hawaii.
- In areas of great physical beauty and good climate, such as the Pacific Northwest and Colorado and central and western North Carolina. These contrast with areas of urban deterioration, such as once around the University of Chicago and still around Columbia.

The above illustrations on the positive side seem to cover much of the United States, but actually they leave out more territory than they include. As I count them, something over half of the research universities, according to the Carnegie classification system, are now located in presumably less advantaged areas as against the apparently more favored.

Let me note that some institutions do rise above their "natural level" given their geographical locations. An illustration is Madison. It was once (1925) rated in the top half-dozen. Geographical location did not favor it all that much. It rose rapidly at the time of the progressive movement in Wisconsin, led by the La Follettes and the populist leadership of Van Hise as president of the university, who believed that "the borders of the campus are the boundaries of the state." Madison became a truly cosmopolitan intellectual center, drawing scholars from Europe and the East Coast; politically, Wisconsin became the precursor of the national New Deal—the first "brain trust" was composed of Madison professors advising the state government. Madison rose above both its general geographical location (although it has, of course, a spectacular immediate physical setting) and the economic resources of its state—a great historic feat of self-levitation.

The How of Changes

When I was chancellor at Berkeley and then president of the University of California—with a special responsibility for three new campuses—I was heavily involved in the recruitment and retention of faculty members. I learned a great deal by observing our competitors.

My greatest surprise was Indiana University in Bloomington. It kept a few people we wanted, and it took at least one person we badly wanted to keep. I had never been there and made a special three-day trip to see what it had going for it in the countryside of southern Indiana—of all places. It had a lot:

- An excellent library, very well administered
- A fantastic cultural program, particularly music and opera, just down the street from where you lived if you were a faculty member
- An acknowledgment that it could not be good across-the-board but that it could be excellent in carefully chosen fields
- The beauty of the campus, with its groves of trees, and the neighboring forests and hills of Brown County
- The astute and persuasive leadership of Herman Wells—all this in the midst of the surrounding cornfields and hog pens

Princeton was also tougher competition than I expected—an historic university in a beautiful small town and well situated on the eastern seaboard commuting routes to New York and Washington—but more than that. It had flexible resources, and plenty of them, administered adroitly by Dean Douglas Brown. Whatever special opportunity a faculty member or a possible new recruit wanted, Doug Brown could pull it out of his bottomless bag of tricks—a certain house owned by the university to live in, an annual trip to a museum in Rome, a renovated laboratory, an expanded book collection in the Firestone Library. At the University of California, by contrast, whatever we gave to one we had to give to all; at Princeton, it was one by one, and Doug Brown mostly won.

Harvard was no surprise. It was our chief competitor for talent. The more I learned about it, however, the more my respect grew and grew and grew. In particular, I marveled at how, as the nation's oldest university, it was the newest in responding the most quickly to out-front developments in the intellectual world; at how careful it was in its national and international search for persons for tenured positions, with the president personally participating in every search and every appointment ("Is this the best person in the world available to us?"); and at how determined it was to keep a numerical balance between younger and older faculty members, with a rapid turnover of junior fellows competing for tenure. Harvard will always be at the top. I was also impressed by these:

- Stanford—the central role it played in the silicon revolution, and the leadership of Wallace Sterling as president and Fred Terman as provost
- Stanford and Berkeley—how friendly local campuses (like Harvard and MIT, also) can reinforce each other
- Minnesota—the appeal of the surrounding community, with its respect for intellectual pursuits, with its cultural facilities, with its traditions of civility and good citizenship
- Michigan—the intensity of statewide support for what was the first of the great state universities; the loyalty of its faculty members to the institution; the provision of lump-sum financing by the state government within the framework of constitutional autonomy; the desire and ability (via lump-sum grants) to seek excellence in all fields across-the-board; and its constant "mainstream" orientation
- Michigan State—how well it played the political strengths of its central role in agriculture; how quickly and effectively it participated in the new opportunities made available by the federal government to build buildings and to engage in research and service activities around the world; and how successfully it used football to gain national visibility—all under the aggressive leadership of John Hannah
- Chicago—the way it employed its lack of a salary structure to outbid others for the persons it wanted to keep by saving money on those it did not; its successful efforts to renovate its surrounding community; the extraordinary devotion and good judgment of its board of trustees; the liveliness of the intellectual debates at the faculty club—the most intense, and at the highest level of discourse, I have ever witnessed anywhere around the academic world
- Madison and Chapel Hill and Lincoln—how unhappy and fearful some faculty members can become at flagship campuses when surrounded administratively by less research-oriented campuses intent on homogenization
- Colorado and Texas and Hawaii—how these great research universities could have been even better if state politics had been less of an historical handicap
- Washington, D.C.—how so many universities each have wanted to be in the "top ten" and how no one, as yet, has been able to break clearly out of the pack in an area where one would expect that there would be at least one university actually in the top ten; somewhat the same observation can be made, also, for Atlanta and for Florida
- CCNY—how the drastic lowering of admission requirements can affect the entire institution (one that was once the greatest source of future Ph.D.'s, along with Berkeley and Illinois)

- Several places—how buying a few "stars," not fully integrated into the campus, and nothing else, ends up in a few "stars" and nothing else
- Tsukuba in Japan—how the wise selection of fields to emphasize can elevate an institution (at Tsukuba: electronics, energy sources, new industrial materials, and business administration for worldwide employment)

Turning now to the University of California when Berkeley came to be rated as "the best balanced distinguished university in the country";[5] when UCLA entered the top ten; and when San Diego came to be on the edge of the top twenty; I note:

- The improvement by one-half in the formula negotiated with the state for support of the libraries, and the concentration of the resulting financial support on three libraries (Berkeley, UCLA, and San Diego)—rather than across-the-board—with union catalogues and intercampus bus services to make all holdings readily available on the several campuses, (and with the libraries at Berkeley and UCLA now rated as number two and number three in the nation, after Harvard as number one, by the Association of Research Libraries)
- The central role played by the academic senate on each campus, as pioneered by Berkeley, in assuring high-quality additions to the tenured faculty with common oversight of *all* departments and *all* professional schools and colleges
- The advantages of a lump-sum budget from Sacramento that made possible improvements in *all* sectors of a campus, one or a few at a time, versus segmented budgets for "each tub on its own bottom"
- The importance of the quality of departmental and school leadership, and of central campus policies that concentrated new faculty positions now in one department and now in another as efforts were made sequentially to raise their status, and that associated the selection of strong department chairs and deans with this concentration of new positions
- The advancement in the quality of cultural programs and of departments in the visual and performing arts for their own sake, but also as assets to the entire campus more generally and particularly in recruiting new faculty members and their spouses
- The policies of giving UCLA equal opportunity to advance along with Berkeley rather than continuing it as the "southern branch"; of giving San Diego special opportunities to ascend as an outstanding research university matching the superb recruiting skills of Roger Revelle; and of giving the San Francisco Health Sciences campus the support it needed in an internal battle to move from a more traditional approach to medicine to a more modern and scientific orientation (with it consequently jumping into the top four)

• The decentralization of daily decision making to the individual campuses within a competitive atmosphere and with an emphasis on each campus developing its own distinctive personality

Prospects for 1990–2010

What does this all mean for the 1990s? The possibility of more changes up and down than usual; thus more like 1870–1900 or 1960–80. Probably more of a role for the states, and particularly for their governors, in determining what happens among public institutions; and for the federal government with its distribution of large-scale research projects among both public and private institutions. Much will also depend on regional developments, with advancing communities aiding their universities—as in Atlanta and Pittsburgh, each with two universities rising rapidly in receipt of federal "academic science" funds. But university policies and campus leadership will continue also to have major roles to play, as always in the past, with particular attention to presidents and to faculty leadership.

The pride of the old and the aspirations of the new will be in constant conflict, and sometimes one and sometimes the other will win out. There will be conflict, too, between diversity and excellence in the faculty, a conflict some places will handle better than others. Consequential dramas are now starting to be played on the many stages of research and other doctorate-granting universities and at a quickening pace.[6]

In particular, I would note the possibility of a "quickening pace" for some universities in the South and Southwest. Of the six states whose research and doctorate-granting universities increased their R&D spending by 100 percent or more in 1984–89, five are in the South.[7] Georgia Tech's rise has been particularly rapid in R&D expenditures. It rose from sixty-seventh to twenty seventh between 1972 and 1987. Also spectacular have been the rise of Texas A&M and Texas-Austin. The same National Science Foundation report also notes the rise of North Carolina–Chapel Hill into the top twenty in reputational rankings for the first time in 1982.[8]

Postscript: Notations on the Other Twenty-two Hundred

What about the 2,200 ("nonspecialized") institutions that are *not* research or other doctorate-granting universities, but that combine for 70 percent of all enrollments? Most of them are also in competitive situations, though these vary in the degrees of their intensity. Few of the 2,200 match, however, the intensity of the research and doctorate-granting universities in competitive endeavors. The reasons for this high degree of intense competition among research institutions include their large size and their better-known names, as well as their participation in nationwide, or at least regionwide, competitive activities, including athletics. Also—and very important—there are readily available measures to indicate success, particularly in the obtaining of research grants from federal agencies. Additionally, their faculty members, in the process of selection, tend to be highly entreprenurial types.

The next most competitive group is composed of the more selective liberal arts colleges (Liberal Arts I colleges—about 150 institutions), institutions that also operate within a nationwide, or at least extensive regionwide, context, and where they, too, have a widely used index of relative success: the SAT (and ACT) scores of the entering students they attract.

But all institutions, within their categories and within their relevant geographical regions, compete for students, for funds, for reputation. It is, overall, the most competitive system of higher education in the world. Private fund-raising by both public and private institutions has in recent times increasingly become a mechanism for competitive advantage.

There are at least two special situations. One is that, of the comprehensive colleges and universities (about 450 institutions), most are intent on "upward drift." They have a less distinctive mission and constitute a more in-between category than any of the others. Many within this category would like to move up into the doctorate-granting category. Most of their faculty members have doctorates from research or other doctorate-granting institutions. In moving "down" to employment at the comprehensive level, some act as though they inhabit a graveyard of disappointed expectations. Doctorate-granting status also brings, generally, lower teaching loads, higher salaries, more travel funds, and better library facilities. The regrettably low status of teaching in higher education gives faculty members less reward from the activity than they would expect to gain from research, and it is very hard for individuals to make a visible mark in teaching, since its quality is less subject to rating.

The other special situation is "survival drift." This particularly affects the less selective liberal arts colleges (Liberal Arts II colleges—about 600 institutions), which have been shifting in the direction of more comprehensive institutions as they add more vocational majors in an effort to sustain their operations.[9] Once again, some do better than others.

The community colleges (1,050 institutions) compete more for generalized "reputation" than to advance in specific tests of level of rankings—there is a well-established group of elite institutions. Most community colleges have local markets for students and more nearly local sources of funding, factors that reduce the areas of competition.

All of these several categories of institutions face many of the same problems—the same unusually high turnover of faculty members over the next twenty years, for example. All of them, in responding, are also affected by their geographical locations, but in quite differing degrees. The community colleges, and the less selective liberal arts colleges, in particular, are dependent on their situations, including the changing natures of their surrounding communities—for many of them, location, by itself, is decisive to the course of their development.

I have the impression that institutions in these two categories are also particularly affected by the performances of their presidents in relation to their surrounding communities. There are, consequently, a larger proportion of both presidential heroes and failures in these two types of institutions—the most demanding leadership environments of all—than anywhere else.

I also have the impression that boards of trustees make more of a difference in these two categories, and particularly in the community colleges. Their boards are often quite small, and the members often have short terms. Such boards can therefore experience significant changes in their conduct, almost overnight. By contrast, some other types of institutions are more dependent on the quality of their faculty governance (which also varies but within a narrower range): Faculty governance is particularly decisive in the most academically elite research universities and liberal arts colleges.

Those institutions most dependent on their changing local communities, on their changing presidents and boards, and on a limited range of program offerings are more likely to move up and down more rapidly in their reputations. Those institutions more dependent on national developments, on faculty governance, and on a wide range of activities are likely to change rank order more slowly.

As a consequence of all the above observations and speculations, it may be said that competition is endemic in American higher education, but that the rules of the game, the layouts and conditions of the playing fields, the composition of the teams, and the methods of keeping score all vary enormously from one segment of higher education to another. The vigor of the competition also varies from time to time, but, in the times just ahead, it will be especially vigorous across all of higher education.

Notes

This chapter is reprinted from *Change* 23, no. 3 (May-June 1991): 8–15. Reprinted with permission of the Helen Dwight Reid Educational Foundation. Published by Heldref Publications, 1319 18th Street, N.W., Washington, D.C. 20036-1802. Copyright 1991.

1. Robert S. McIntyre, "Tax Inequality Caused Our Ballooning Budget Deficit," *Challenge* 34, no. 6 (November-December 1991): 26.

2. The categories of institutions follow the Carnegie classification system.

3. Added to this list might be Rockefeller University, which metamorphosed (unofficially in 1954 and officially in 1965) from the Rockefeller Institute for Medical Research (founded in 1901) into Rockefeller University.

4. It has been estimated that, from the two causes taken together from 1990 to 2010, there will be 563,000 new appointments as against 663,000 current faculty total (Howard R. Bowen and Jack H. Schuster, *American Professors: A National Resource Imperiled* [New York: Oxford University Press, 1986]). It has been estimated that, within arts and sciences over the period from 1992 to 2012, there will be 153,000 new appointments as against 154,000 current faculty at four-year institutions (William G. Bowen and Julie Ann Sosa, *Prospects for Faculty in the Arts and Sciences* [Princeton: Princeton University Press, 1989]).

5. Allan M. Cartter, *An Assessment of Quality in Graduate Education* (Washington, D.C.: American Council on Education, 1966), 107.

6. The institutions that have improved their positions most in receipt of federal "academic science" funds from 1979 to 1988 are as follows:

East—6 (two of them in Pittsburgh):
    Boston University
    Carnegie-Mellon
    University of Massachusetts–Amherst
    State University of New York–Stony Brook
    University of Pittsburgh
    University of Vermont
South—4 (two of them in Atlanta):
    Emory University
    Georgia Tech
    Louisiana State University
    Vanderbilt
West—6:
    University of Arizona
    University of California–Irvine
    University of Colorado
    New Mexico State University
    University of California–Santa Barbara
    Utah State University
Midwest—3:
    University of Cincinnati
    Indiana University–Bloomington
    University of Michigan

(Calculated from National Science Foundation, *Federal Support to Universities, Colleges, and Selected Non-Profit Institutions,* Fiscal Year 1979 and Fiscal Year 1988.)

7. These states are Alabama, Florida, North Carolina, South Carolina, and Tennessee ("Fact File: Spending for Research and Development by Doctorate-Granting

Universities [by state, fiscal year 1989]," *The Chronicle of Higher Education* 37, no. 18 [16 January 1991]: A31).

8. National Science Foundation, *The State of Academic Science and Engineering*, NSF 90-35 (1990), 99–100.

9. See David W. Breneman, "Are We Losing Our Liberal Arts Colleges?" *College Board Review*, no. 156 (Summer 1990): 16–21ff.

Epilogue: On Facing the Unknown

It was one kind of world for higher education when three dynamic forces were working strongly together (fast-rising enrollments, fast-rising resources, and fast-rising needs of society for new and better kinds of service) as they did for most of the past century. It will be still another kind of world if and when only the rising needs of society conduce toward dynamic change.

But higher education should not be too fearful. Once higher education feared that "more is worse"; now it is beginning to fear that "less is worse." However, it is destined, in a world led by knowledge, to be an ever more important element of society. Whether with more or fewer enrollments and resources, higher education is tied to a secular trend that began with the Academy and Lyceum, and that may last at least as long into the future as they now lie in the past, and that is to be ever more central.

I end this attempt to anticipate some aspects of the near future with a notation of my greatest current concerns after having participated in higher education as a faculty member, administrator, and commentator for now nearly half a century:

Higher education has not yet enlarged its vision to include the creation of a "nation of educated people,"[1] as Howard Bowen suggested it should.

Much more should be done to find talent in all segments of society, particularly among underserved minorities.

Too little responsibility is being taken by higher education for assisting all of youth in making the difficult transition into adult life, and not just those within the walls of our colleges and universities.

Undergraduates are not being given a reasonable opportunity to engage in a broad learning experience along with their specializations.

Higher education is becoming too unbalanced in the direction of serving the economy.

Too little organized thought is being directed toward the great issues of industrialized society.

The sense of community on campus is being lost as more faculty members conduct themselves as nomads and more students as members of tribes.

Institutions are neglecting, at their peril, ethical considerations in both their internal conduct and their external relations.

Merit may be unduly diluted by the emphasis on seniority and on proportionality at the more advanced levels of higher education.

Differentiation of function may slowly erode before the forces supporting homogenization.

The "estates" into which campuses are divided may increasingly lose consideration for each other, and presidents and trustees may be in an increasingly weaker position to hold them all together.

Too many states and coordinating mechanisms are too "line-item" focused in their forms of control. Guidance through setting missions and financing on the basis of general formulas is the better course of development.

Higher education in the United States may fare less well than it needs to in the increasingly worldwide competition for excellence.

Institutions of higher education are not enough concerned with effective use of resources and are not well organized to consider such use. Too many decisions are made at levels far removed from direct contact with external financial pressures.

Higher education may lose some of its dynamism in service to society as growth slows and as internal conflicts accelerate at a time when there is still so much to be done.

This is a substantial list, but higher education in the United States has an even more substantial list of past accomplishments. It has

- provided more access to young persons than in any other nation
- made available to these students a wider range of choices than anywhere else
- at its best, at the Ph.D. level, offered training of the highest quality
- met labor-market requirements quickly and fully
- become the dominant single center for research in the world
- developed an effective system of shared governance as best set forth in the policy standards of the American Association of University Professors
- drawn forth a high level of financial support from the public
- justified, by its conduct, state coordination mostly by general guidance
- made available to society more forms of services beyond those rendered in most other nations

The United States has, overall, the most effective system of higher education the world has ever known.

Bertrand Russell once wrote that "the important fact of the present time is not the struggle between capitalism and socialism but the struggle between industrial civilization and humanity."[2] Higher education has been on both sides of this latter struggle, but more on the side of humanity. Unfortunately, however, in some important respects humanity has been losing, as in, for example, protection of the environment and care for all children and youth. The struggle continues, however, and higher education is an increasingly more important participant as it adds new knowledge and higher skills.

Notation 1, on a Disjunction: Ex post versus ex ante Views of History

Higher education seems always to be celebrating its glorious past, which gets more glorious all the time, and fearing its dreadful future, which appears more dreadful all the time. I recently attended a conference in connection with the hundredth anniversary of the founding of the University of Chicago—a university that really does have a glorious past. One of the major papers,[3] on "external and internal threats" to the university, even suggested that universities might go the way of the monasteries of the sixteenth century in England, having outlived their usefulness. The university is becoming an "arm of the state" and also an arm of industry externally, and too bureaucratized internally.

My own university—the University of California—is preparing for its 125th anniversary (in 1993). It will look back at its golden age since the end of World War II—at all those Nobel Prize winners (just as Chicago looked back at its own), at Berkeley being rated the "best balanced distinguished university"[4] in the United States, at UCLA entering the top ten, at San Diego entering the top twenty (the only one in that group to be founded in the twentieth century), at the San Francisco Medical Center entering the top four, at the accomplishment of the Master Plan for Higher Education in California, and at much else. This will be the way it looks ex post. But I also saw this history unfold ex ante—the fear that we would be engulfed by the GI rush, that the Senator McCarthy period in American politics and our own dreadful oath controversy would sink the university into being a has-been, that the "tidal wave" of students would really drown us, that the student revolts (which we did not entirely escape) would be the end of all we held dear, that the election of an unfriendly governor and the series of depressions in the 1970s would starve us of resources, that the demographic depression of the 1980s would depress us as never before. We were almost always fearing something. Now it is the difficult financial situation of the state of California and internal divisions over curricular policy and the composition of new faculty appointments. But in 1993 we will be rejoicing after 125 years of a triumphant series of successes!

Why are we always so happy looking backward and so unhappy looking forward? I do not fully understand.

Notation 2: On Optimism and Pessimism in Anticipating the Future

Once upon a time on at least one issue we were too optimistic. We thought that the impacts of past racism could be fully overcome by the end of this century. They will not be. We thus established an expectation of performance that we failed to meet. But much has been accomplished. About one-third of our black citizens are in middle-income occupations, largely through their use of higher education, including the colleges founded for blacks, which have been such a great national asset. We were once excessively optimistic. This has led now to excessive disappointments.

Once an unreserved optimist about American higher education, I now have reservations. But I still totally oppose unreserved pessimism as self-defeating and as disowned by historical experience. I have come to support pessimism about the short-run future and optimism about the long run. This combination has two advantages. One is personal satisfaction. In the short run, there may be pleasant surprises. And in the long-run (provided the long run is defined as a long-enough period) there will be as yet no actually realized disappointments and only hopes still to be realized. The other advantage is operational usefulness. Concern for the short-run future is almost always justified, for higher education does most of the time face new challenges, and they are better met if thoughtful concern turns into progressive solutions. High expectations for the long run are also mostly justified; and these expectations add motivation, and their realization in past times adds confidence.[5] Short-run productive pessimism can help create the basis for long-run optimistic results.

A "time of troubles" almost certainly now lies ahead for higher education in the United States, but then it almost always has when viewed ex ante. The chances are, however, that higher education not only will once again survive but will be in a position to contribute even more to the life of society.

I acknowledge at least one law of human behavior—Goethe's law: "Man makes mistakes for as long as he keeps on striving" (Faust, speaking in "Prologue in Heaven").

I also acknowledge one law of education—Plato's law: "The wheel of education once set in motion moves at an ever faster pace." True in Ancient Greece. Not true in the Dark Ages. True and ever truer in modern times. The basic question about the future is where that law will have taken us by the end of the next century.

Notation 3: An Advancing Source of Pessimism—May 1993

Earlier in these discussions of "Troubled Times" I identified (p. 151) the racial crisis as the most likely dominant theme of the 1990s. Now I am not so sure. The recession of the early 1990s continues its slow course of recovery. The Great Productivity Stagnation that began in the 1970s is about to enter its third decade. New demands for public resources assert themselves as for health care as the population ages, and for child and youth care as the family disintegrates. As a consequence, the nation faces a confrontation over the use of resources as never before in its history—private versus public uses, and one public use versus another. And, thus far, public institutions of higher education have been losing. By recent count, public colleges and universities in thirty-six states have been assessed budget cuts over the past two years. By contrast, some private institutions, as shown in their recent endowment drives, have been greatly advantaged by the enormous shift of net income since 1980 to the wealthiest elements of the population— in the hundreds of billions of dollars.

Thus, far, public higher education has responded mostly with short-run politically motivated adjustments (as it did in the early 1970s)—for example, reductions in plant maintenance and book acquisitions where there are no immediate constituencies to be aroused. But the challenge now is almost certain to be longer run and more drastic for public higher education than in the early 1970s or even in the Great Depression, and politically cost-free cuts are in short supply. At the time of the Great Depression, there were half a million students in public higher education to be financed, now there are more nearly 12 million. Then the cost of living went down (by 25 percent), now it goes up. Then there was a modest increase in enrollments, now we face Tidal Wave II (the grandchildren of the GIs), starting in 1997 and ending not before 2010, which will be as great in absolute numbers (but not percentage increases) as Tidal Wave I.

Pressures for reduction in expenditures will concentrate decision making at the levels of boards of trustees and presidents internally, and governors and legislatures externally. It will also concentrate dissatisfaction directed at those levels as schools and departments and institutes and individual faculty members seek to preserve their support, and, on occasion, their actual survival. The total level of dissatisfaction may never have been greater in what has been, by and large, a very satisfied segment of American society.

Fiscal scrutiny from above will invade historic enclaves of freedom of choice and action. Autonomy at the level of operating units will be a great loser, but only after many rearguard defensive actions. Specifically, a further "flight from teaching" will be endangered. Higher education has never been a highly cost-conscious enterprise, and, within it, the decentralized units that make the expenditures are often far removed from participation in the battles to secure the resources—those who spend the money mostly do not have to fight to get it (except in research contracts). Now cost-consciousness will be pushed down the hierarchy.

Situations will vary greatly from state to state, as the American economy undergoes a great restructuring and some states gain and some lose—and so will their systems of higher education.

The great test for public higher education, overall and state by state, will be to preserve both access and quality to the extent that can be done. These will be the two bottom lines. What to sacrifice?

This is a sad note of pessimism on which to conclude.

The optimistic counternote is that, in the longer run, the secular trend for higher education must be ever upward. There is light at the end of the tunnel. But the tunnel may turn out to be twenty years long for public higher education (1990–2010). Only a return of high prosperity and/or of a higher rate of productivity increases, as from 1945 to 1970 (3 percent per year versus the current average of 1 percent), can shorten the length of that tunnel of "troubled times."

Notes

1. Howard R. Bowen, *The State of the Nation and the Agenda for Higher Education* (San Francisco: Jossey-Bass, 1982).

2. Bertrand Russell, *The Prospects of Industrial Civilization* (New York: Century, 1923), Preface.

3. By Michael Shattock of the University of Warwick—a highly respected commentator on British higher education ("The Internal and External Threats to the University of the Twenty-first Century," *Minerva* 30, no. 2 [Summer 1992]: 130–47).

4. Allan M. Cartter, *An Assessment of Quality in Graduate Education* (Washington, D.C.: American Council on Education, 1966), 107.

5. Note that sixty of the seventy-five institutions in Europe founded before 1520 still doing much the same things and in the same places are universities. They, among all institutions, have most nearly had eternal life (Clark Kerr, *Higher Education Cannot Escape History: Conflicts and Contradictions* [Albany: State University of New York Press, 1994], chap. 3, table 1).

Index